D1514730

THE ILLUSTRATED BOOK OF
MAGIC TRICKS

THE
ILLUSTRATED BOOK OF
MAGIC TRICKS

BY

WILL DEXTER

MEMBER OF THE INNER MAGIC CIRCLE

ILLUSTRATED BY STAN LANE

ABBEY   LIBRARY

LONDON

Copyright © Murrays Sales and Service Co.

PUBLISHED BY
THE ABBEY LIBRARY

Cresta House
146-152 Holloway Road, London N. 7

PRINTED IN ROMANIA

CONTENTS

	Page
Introduction	7
That wonderful wand	9
This is a magic wand	10
Who's knocking, it must be spirits	11
Big wand from tiny purse	12
Presto! It's gone	13
The ghostly pencil	14
The lazy match	15
Where there's smoke	16
The anti-gravity matches	17
The ghostly match boxes	18
A light from your pocket	19
Sweet—and hot!	20
Vapour of the Yogi	21
The floating candle	22
The feast of candles!	23
A double-headed coin!	24
Where does the money go?	25
Who has the money?	26
Through the fourth dimension!	27
Your coin, Sir!	28
Guess which!	29
A valuable coin sleight	30
1-2-3! Gone	31
Robbers and sheep	33
The homing coins	35
Coin passing	37

	Page
Bank balance	39
Or—How to spend your money—and yet keep it	40
The melting coin	41
Cash—with care	42
Into thin air!	43
Out of thin air!	44
Penny in the bun	45
The bank note machine	46
The secrets of palming	47
Remember these card magic terms	49
The false shuffle	50
Card control!	51
X marks the spot!	53
Another card force	54
The glide	55
2 out of 52	56
The turnover card	57
The famous 4-ace trick	59
The marvellous stripper pack!	61
The world's longest trick!	63
And I shuffled the cards myself!	64
Something up your sleeve	65
The boomerang	66
The card on the wall	68
The card through the table	66
Five choices	70

	Page		Page
The card with four sides!	71	The human clock	107
Strong man stuff!	72	Colour sense	108
The Romans had a word for it!	73	The silent spelling bee	109
Jumping colours	75	Two for the price of one	110
The magic circlet	76	Special edition! Extra!	111
The obedient orange	77	The rajah's jewels	113
The cube and frame	78	Can you believe your eyes?	114
The snap knot	80	Dice deception	115
A trick with Polo—the mint with the hole!	81	I only cheat a little	116
Almost the Indian rope trick!	82	The baffling banana	117
The indestructible rope!	83	You can—they can't	118
Going up!	84	The super ring vanish	119
Through the tunnel	85	The ring and the ball of wool	120
The string and the straw	86	Full—empty!	122
This reef knot is a slip-knot!	87	The topsy-turvy bottle	123
The knot that's not!	88	Solid water!	124
A Houdini escape	89	A quart into a pint pot	125
The great sack escape!	90	The sands of the desert	126
Robin Hood escapes again	91	Water becomes wine!	127
The electronic brain	92	The restless ball	128
Ghost in the parlour	94	Dry water—by magic!	129
The spirits tell!	95	Floating sugar	130
The psychometric boxes	96	Phantom smoke	131
The number you want!	97	Atomic bubbles	132
A baffling book mystery	98	Magic springtime	133
The dictionary test	99	The human power plant	134
The domino mystery	100	The colour-changing balloon	135
The spirit writes!	101	The ghosts' gallery	136
Mathematical mystery	102	What? No juice?	137
More mysterious maths	103	The confetti tube	139
The sidereal pendulum	104	The spirits box	141
The mystery of the four marbles	105	The chest of the genii	142
Ears at your finger tips!	106	The rabbit out of the hat	143

Introduction

THE FIRST magic book I ever read was called *The Modern Conjurer*. It's an old book, with lots and lots of pictures in it. I learnt more magic from those pictures than I've ever learnt since. The Chinese have a proverb: "One picture is worth a thousand words." That's very true, especially of magic.

And so the artist and I have compiled this book of pictorial magic for you, believing that if you study it carefully, and learn the tricks in it, you'll become a good conjurer.

Some of the tricks are new. Some are good old ones which have entertained and amused audiences for many, many years. Some are easy, and some are a little more difficult. *But all of them need practice, however easy they seem*. That's the very first secret of magic—PRACTICE.

And the next most important secret is—KEEP YOUR SECRETS! Don't ever tell anyone how a trick is done. You've had to *learn* the way to do it; let other people do likewise!

If you learn how to do only one single trick out of all this book, bear in mind those two important principles: PRACTICE . . . and KEEP YOUR SECRETS!

When you feel that you can present several of these tricks with confidence and assurance, then look around for other books on magic. Learn all you can from books. And then make friends with other conjurers and exchange your information. But remember—only swop tricks with conjurers! Everybody else must think that these things are done by magic!

Good luck—and happy conjuring!

WILL DEXTER

London, 1957.

THAT WONDERFUL WAND!

IT'S MORE USEFUL THAN YOU MIGHT THINK! THE MAGICIAN'S WAND IS USED FOR MISDIRECTION AS WELL AS TO PROVIDE VALUABLE SECRET AID WHEN YOU NEED IT

The wand is usually made of black wood or plastic, with white or silver ends. But —

— if you want to be a little more original, you may like to use a Chinese chopstick (which you can buy from the Chinese Arts and Crafts shops, or from novelty shops) made of ivory, plastic, or rare Oriental woods.

Or you will find that this unusual wand, made from 15 inches of malacca cane, will interest your audience, and be easy and pleasant to handle.

Remember! whichever type of wand you use, your audience will like to believe that it's the wand that makes the magic!

This is a MAGIC wand!

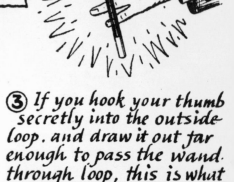

SO MAGICAL THAT IT CLINGS
TO YOUR HAND WITHOUT ANY
VISIBLE MEANS OF SUPPORT!

HERE'S YOUR SECRET —

① *You'll need some fine black silk thread and a needle and — a flat lead fishing weight with a small ring attached.*

③ *If you hook your thumb secretly into the outside loop, and draw it out far enough to pass the wand through loop, <u>this</u> is what you can do!*

② *Thread the needle, and pass it through the top of the trousers at Ⓐ. Pass needle through ring on weight, and then out through top of trousers at Ⓑ. Knot ends of thread together, so that a loop of about 18 inches hangs inside trousers. Pull knot to inside of trousers to hide it. Now you have a 3 inch loop <u>outside</u> trousers, and weight hangs on an 18 inch loop <u>inside</u> trouser leg.*

The weight keeps the thread taut and allows you to move the wand freely.

Experiment well with this secret! You'll find you can also suspend the wand from other objects — books, two pencils, etc., as well as changing it from hand to hand.

10

Who's knocking?
IT MUST BE SPIRITS

AT LEAST, THAT'S WHAT
YOUR AUDIENCE WILL
THINK WHEN YOUR
WAND BEATS A
RAT-TAT-TAT
ON YOUR TABLE!

(1) But we know it's not spirits, don't we? Because this is what we've done to make the wand rap out it's weird message :—

(2) The two candlesticks are important! A _fine black_ thread is tied to candle (A), and runs through an eyelet on candle (B). Thence, the thread runs off-stage to a hidden assistant, who pulls it gently when necessary. The wand rests on edge of tray and it's end lies on the thread.

(3) If you wish to dispense with a hidden assistant, tie the other end of the thread to a chair, and press body gently against it.

Press against thread here

HEAVY candlesticks, please!

A B

Thread runs through eyelet on candle (B), eyelet on table and a third eyelet on floor to hidden assistant in wings →

11

BIG WAND
FROM TINY PURSE!

> **CARRY YOUR 15" WAND IN A 3" PURSE!**

HERE'S THE SECRET:—

①  Cut a 1½" hole in one end of the purse. Close purse and put it in your right coat pocket.

Hole

② Wand is hidden in left sleeve. A rubber band around wrist holds end of wand in place till needed.

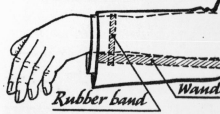

Rubber band   Wand

③ Take purse from pocket with right hand, and show it casually without opening it or revealing hole in end. Hold left hand ready to receive purse, and take it from right hand.

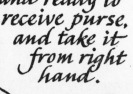

④ Right hand opens purse, and right forefinger and thumb go through hole to draw wand out of sleeve and through the purse —S-L-O-W-L-Y!

PLEASE NOTE! →

MIRROR PRACTICE NEEDED!

PRESTO! IT'S GONE!

This handkerchief vanish was a favourite trick of that great master of magic, David Devant

A silk handkerchief — a sheet of newspaper — and a wand provide the mystery

1

The silk is pushed into the newspaper, which has been rolled into a cone. The cone is then closed at the top.

2 When a spectator opens the paper cone, the silk has vanished!

The wand is a hollow one, containing a thin steel rod, which is secretly pulled out when wand is first pushed into cone. The rod is left in cone. Handkerchief is draped over rod, and hollow wand is placed over rod & pushed down. Silk is forced into the hollow wand, and rod is left in position and taken out of cone inside the wand.

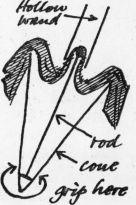

Hollow wand

rod
cone
grip here

The GHOSTLY Pencil

When you take this pencil out of your pocket and drop it in a bottle, it climbs slowly out again!

The Secret is—

a long hair or very fine thread attached to the pocket where you carry the pencil. The other end is secured to the blunt end of the pencil with a small dab of beeswax.

When you hand the pencil to your astonished friends, don't forget to scrape off the dab of beeswax and detach the thread!

COCA COLA

When you press your hand at Ⓧ and tighten the thread (in 'mesmerising' the pencil!) the pencil is slowly drawn up & out of the bottle.

The Lazy Match

It lights when you strike it but it just won't stay lit!

This is the

SECRET

Paint a broad ring of **SODIUM SILICATE** round match just below the head & let it dry.

The match will light but will go out immediately!

SODIUM SILICATE

Sodium Silicate is also known as **WATERGLASS.** Buy it from your chemist.

Where there's smoke....

... there's <u>no</u> fire this time! Here's another good trick with matches.

Strike them as carefully as you will, these matches will only produce smoke — But there's lots of that!

THE SECRET

SODIUM SILICATE

Waterglass again!

Soak the heads of <u>safety</u> matches in **SODIUM SILICATE**, and let them dry for several hours.
Matches treated in this way will splutter and smoke when struck on the box.

The Anti-Gravity Matches

Although you turn the tray of a full box of matches upside down, the matches don't fall out until you say the **MAGIC WORD!** — **WHY?**

Because, although you can open the box and show the matches, the tray has been faked

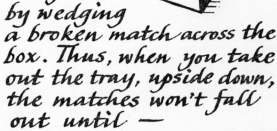

by wedging a broken match across the box. Thus, when you take out the tray, upside down, the matches won't fall out until —

you squeeze the **ends** of the tray.

Then the matches will fall — and the broken, short match is hidden among them as it falls with them!

Short match →

The GHOSTLY match boxes

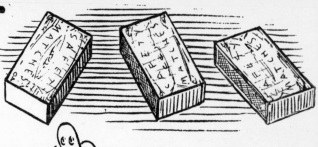

In one of these three match boxes (you tell your audience) you keep a tame **GHOST!**

He is able to jump invisibly from box to box, and nobody can track him to his resting place!

To prove it, you demonstrate that one box, and only one box, rattles. That's where the ghost is — *now*!

This way to THE SECRET!

A fourth match box, containing a heavy marble, is hidden in the right sleeve or fixed to your wrist with a rubber band.

The other boxes are empty. Shake two with the <u>left</u> hand, and they won't rattle. But whenever you shake a box with the <u>right</u> hand, that box will rattle!

But after you've mixed the boxes, nobody can find the one that rattles — the ghost has moved to another box! You can repeat this little trick indefinitely, — but please don't!

18

A LIGHT FROM YOUR POCKET

Whenever you need it! —

THIS WAY TO THE SECRET.

(1) Glue a strip of coarse sandpaper to a 3" strip of cardboard which is folded across the middle —

(2) Lay a match on the sandpaper and fold cardboard over it

(3) Pass a safety pin through the fold and —

(4) slip a thin rubber band over the ends of the folded strip.

(5) Now pin the striker inside your coat pocket and

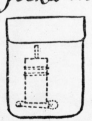

PRESTO! You have only to pull out the match to produce it blazing merrily!

SWEET — AND HOT!

You may not know it, but a lump of sugar is non-inflammable — it just won't burn with a flame. So when your friends see you set a lump of sugar blazing merrily, they'll wonder how you do it.

And when _they_ try to burn a lump of sugar — well, they'll find it completely impossible!

HERE'S THE SECRET ⟶

a small pile of cigarette ash.

Secretly dip a corner of the sugar in the ash and put a match to that corner.

It'll blaze away and splutter merrily!

But REMEMBER! Do your dipping secretly!

VAPOUR OF THE YOGI

A closely-guarded secret of the Eastern wonder-workers is their method of producing smoke from the air and from their finger-tips

HERE IS THE WESTERN MAGICIAN'S WAY OF PERFORMING THIS SPECTACULAR MIRACLE!

① Carefully tear the striking surfaces off several boxes of _safety_ matches

② Burn these on a saucer, and blow away all the ashes

④  This oily film must be carefully scraped off — and stored in a small metal pill box

③  You will find that a brown greasy film is left on the saucer

⑤ Now, if you take a small dab of the oily substance on your finger-tip, and rub your thumb on it, smoke will be produced by the friction

BUT — TAKE CARE — The oily film is POISONOUS!

The Floating Candle

Take away the candlestick, and the lighted candle remains floating in the air with no visible support!

SECRET ➤

lead weight

A fine, strong, blackened wire (a steel guitar string is ideal) is concealed in the coat lining. A small lead weight on the lower end causes the wire to be kept out of sight until the trick starts.

The candle is transfixed on the sharp end of the wire & is drawn up & forward a little, pulling the wire from its hiding place.

At finish, wire is allowed to sink back into coat.

The Feast of Candles!

If you've just done a trick in which a candle is used, you can further astonish your friends by taking the lighted candle from the candlestick and eating it!

(It's very good, too!)

The parlour conjurers of the Victorian days made a great mystery of this baffling trick, which is rarely seen nowadays.

SECRET

① Trim a peeled banana down to a cylindrical shape to make the "candle"

② Stick a slip of almond or brazil nut into the end for the "wick"

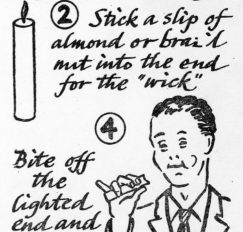

③ Light the slip of nut at the last moment, as the oil in it doesn't burn for many seconds.

④ Bite off the lighted end and close your mouth on it. That will extinguish the flame at once.

MM! DELICIOUS!

EVERY PENNY IS
A DOUBLE-HEADED COIN!

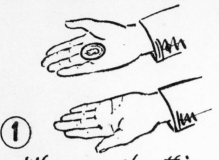

① When you slap this coin — head side up — into your left hand ✓

② There's a head on the other side as well!

But — there isn't really! Still, there's a head showing on each side, so how *is* it done?

Here's a slow-motion explanation —

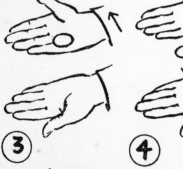

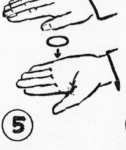

③ Right hand moves quickly, but smoothly from under coin;

④ Coin starts to drop into left hand;

⑤ Right hand turns over; coin has nearly reached left hand now;

⑥ Coin has fallen on left palm, right hand is ready to slap down on it.

—So the coin never really turns over!

24

WHERE <u>DOES</u> THE MONEY GO?

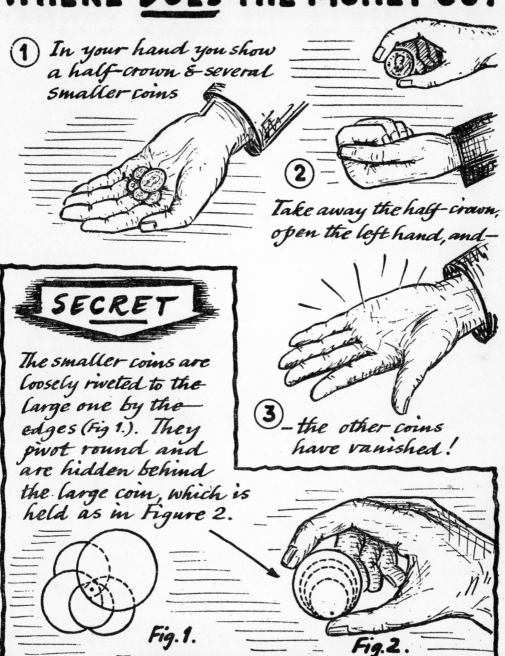

① In your hand you show a half-crown & several smaller coins

② Take away the half-crown, open the left hand, and—

③ —the other coins have vanished!

SECRET

The smaller coins are loosely riveted to the large one by the edges (Fig 1.). They pivot round and are hidden behind the large coin, which is held as in Figure 2.

Fig. 1.

Fig. 2.

MONEY, MONEY,
WHO HAS THE MONEY?

Try this trick with a foreign coin. It looks more unusual — and it prevents your spectators from cheating!

While you are out of the room one spectator is chosen by the rest to hold a coin to his — or her — forehead for 20 seconds. Then, all hands are laid on the table and you are called back into the room.

Your magic wand tells you who has the coin!

SECRET :— The hand which has been held to a forehead will be <u>whiter</u> than all the other hands.

This hand holds the Coin!

And the wand is used — slowly and mysteriously — to point to each hand. When it points to the hand which you noted as being white when you came back to the room (and which will be its normal colour now), make the wand quiver dramatically and tell the person to open that hand and show the coin!

Through the Fourth Dimension!

That's how the coin passes through a borrowed handkerchief!

THIS WAY TO THE FOURTH DIMENSION   THIS WAY TO THE NEXT PAGE

① Hold a penny or other large coin between the left thumb & forefinger.

② coin

Cover coin and hand with the handkerchief.

③ Grip coin & handkerchief firmly at ⊗ and turn coin over towards yourself.

④ Fling handkerchief back over left hand, carefully nipping it against the coin — "to prove that the coin is still there"

⑤ Shake handkerchief forward (coin is now gripped in an _outside_ fold of linen), and twist the handkerchief.

⑥ Keep on twisting, and relax the grip of the left finger & thumb. The coin will slowly be squeezed out of its fold.

⑦ The handkerchief is undamaged, although the coin has passed right through it. It _must_ be the Fourth Dimension — or Magic!

YOUR COIN, SIR!

A number of pennies are gathered from the audience on a tray, & are tipped into a hat. One spectator is then asked to contribute another penny, & to mark it secretly and put it in the hat and shake the coins up.

At once you put your hand in the hat & bring out the marked coin!

SECRET—
The tray is of metal and the coins placed on it become cold quickly

But the secretly marked coin has never been on the tray, and so is still warm from the pocket when it's dropped in the hat.

So all you have to do is feel for the coin that's warmer than the others.

28

GUESS WHICH!

From your pocket you take four coins and four small pill boxes. While your back is turned, the audience cover the coins with the boxes and move them round. When you turn round, you can at once tell which coin is under which box and which way up it is — without lifting the boxes!

SECRET—

← Hair ↗

The coins are two pennies and two florins; one of each has a short, fine hair glued to it. The prepared coins are laid down with the "Tails" side up. The other coins have their "Heads" side up.

Hair →

Hair ↗

NOTE!
You only need move *two* boxes to name *all* coins — a box showing a hair & one that has no hair

When the coins are covered, look for the hairs (A & C boxes in the above sketch). Move one box forward. If it rattles, it contains the florin, which is not as tight a fit as the penny. If it has a hair showing, it's a "Tail"; if no hair, a "Head".

So you can name the coin under any box indicated by the audience, or all the boxes, if you prefer.

29

A VALUABLE COIN SLEIGHT

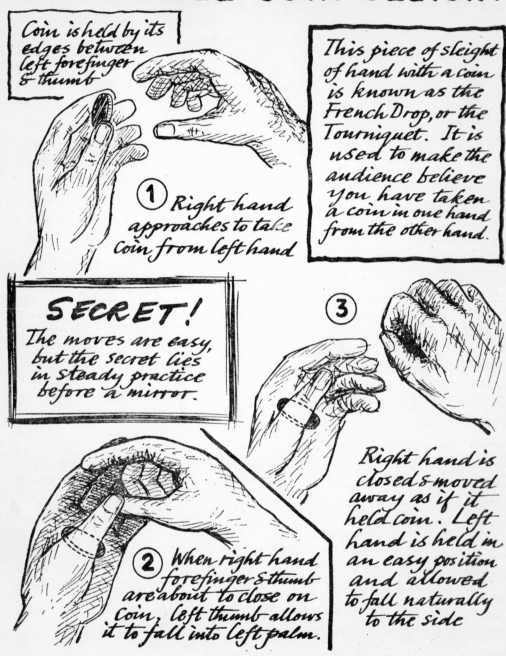

Coin is held by its edges between left forefinger & thumb

① Right hand approaches to take coin from left hand

This piece of sleight of hand with a coin is known as the French Drop, or the Tourniquet. It is used to make the audience believe you have taken a coin in one hand from the other hand.

SECRET!
The moves are easy, but the secret lies in steady practice before a mirror.

③

② When right hand forefinger & thumb are about to close on coin, left thumb allows it to fall into left palm.

Right hand is closed & moved away as if it held coin. Left hand is held in an easy position and allowed to fall naturally to the side

1-2-3! GONE!

This is the vanish of a coin which baffles many conjurers — and yet it's so easy, you can do it first time you try!

1 A penny or other large coin is shown in your right hand

2 You slap it down firmly on to your left hand three times. The third time, you lift your hand — and the coin has gone! And it's *not* up any sleeves!

THE SECRET —

lies in the way you raise the right hand to slap the coin into your left hand

3 Each time you raise the right hand, take it as high as your shoulder, and keep your head bent, the eyes on the *left* hand

4 The last time you raise your right hand, bring it near your collar, and let the coin slip down between your shirt and your neck.

Immediately, bring the right hand down (empty) to slap the left hand as before.

Coin

Conjurers call this "misdirection". The audience, having seen the coin slapped down twice, will watch your *left* hand while the *right* hand does the work!

The Acrobatic Coin —

balances on the tips of the fingers steadily. Then it sways slowly back until it lies flat on the hand. Your audience can lift it off your hand but they'll never find — **THE SECRET!**

HERE IT IS — A PIN!

② Place the coin on the finger-tips and hold it in place with the thumb until the pin is gripped between the fingers.

Hold the pin behind a silver coin with finger and thumb. You can change it from hand to hand safely.

③ When the pin is strongly gripped, raise the thumb, and the coin stands firmly, leaning on the pin

④ Now slowly release the fingers' pressure on the pin allowing the coin to settle back on to the fingers. When it is laid flat, open the fingers slightly and let the pin fall to the ground.

ROBBERS and SHEEP

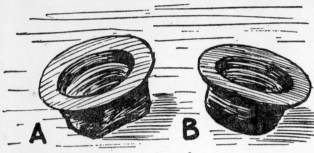

A   B

This is a classic
of conjuring,
using coins or
paper balls.
It's easy but
baffling!
Practise it well!

Two borrowed hats represent
a farmer's barns.

Five pennies
represent five sheep,
and two more pennies
are the robbers ___

A   B

① The robbers each hide
in a barn

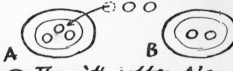

A   B

④ Then it's robber A's
turn again

A   B

② Robber A takes a sheep
into his barn

A   B

⑤ Followed by a sheep for
robber B

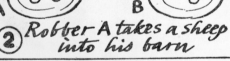

A   B

③ and robber B does
the same

A   B

⑥ The last sheep goes to robber A.
When it's safely in the barn ___

— the robbers hear a policeman coming!

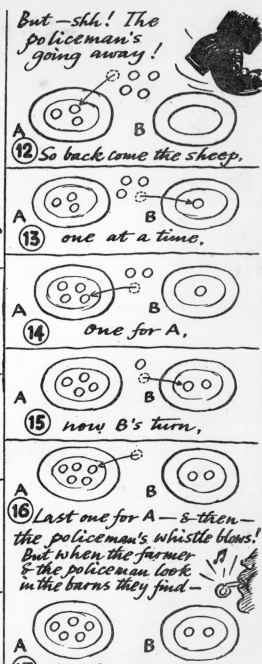

⑫ So back come the sheep,

⑬ one at a time,

⑭ one for A,

⑮ now B's turn,

⑯ Last one for A — & then — the policeman's whistle blows! But when the farmer & the policeman look in the barns they find—

⑰ five sheep in one barn, & the two men in the other!

⑦ So they chase out the sheep one at a time, first robber B.

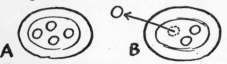

⑧ Then one from robber A,

⑨ Another from B,

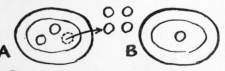

⑩ & another from A and—

⑪ the last one from B.

THE HOMING COINS

Another classic of coin conjuring, made famous years ago by Yank Hoe, an Italian magician in U.S.A.

Four coins, at the corners of a handkerchief, are covered in turn by two cards. One by one, the coins move invisibly to one corner. At the finish of the trick, there are four coins together at one corner. Nobody saw them move—

HOW DID THEY GET THERE ?

SECRET—

—a fifth coin is secretly held in the right-hand finger-palm position. The cards are held in this manner ⟶ when covering the coins. Right-hand card always covers the finger-palmed coin.

① Cards are laid over coins B & C, leaving palmed coin at B. Right hand takes coin from D and takes it under table, pretending to push it through table under corner B, but really palming it.

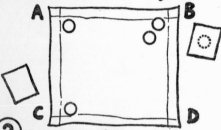

② Cards are lifted to show 2 coins at B. Palmed coin is held under right card (hands omitted in sketch, for clarity)

③ Cards are laid over A & B, and palmed coin is left at B. Right hand takes coin C under table and palms it as in move ①

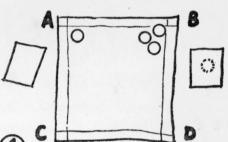

④ Cards are lifted, showing 3 coins now at B. Palmed coin is behind right-hand card.

⑤ Both cards are placed on corner B, leaving palmed coin there. Left hand takes coin from A, and puts it under table to "push it through". Actually, left hand allows coin to slide down trouser-leg into trouser turn-up —

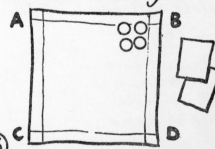

⑥ so that when cards are lifted, all four coins have gathered at corner B — and your hands are empty!

COIN PASSING

Many tricks involve the passing of objects invisibly from one place to another. In this classic of magic, 3 coins pass one at a time from one hand to the other — unseen!

1 Three coins lie in a row at each side of the table.

2 What the audience _don't_ know is that you have a

3 seventh coin palmed in your right hand.

4

5

6

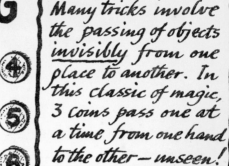

1 Pick up coins 1 & 2 singly and throw into left hand. Pick up coin 3, and throw that into left hand, _at same time releasing palmed coin_ and throwing _both_ coins into left hand. Close left hand tightly.

3 Lay down coins 1, 2, 3 and the secret seventh coin from left hand, & coins 5 & 6 from right hand, retaining coin 4 in right palm.

2 Palm coin 4 when you pick it up with right hand, then pick up coins 5 & 6 and hold in fingers.

4 Repeat move No. 1, secretly throwing palmed coin No. 4, along with another coin, into left hand. Continue to pick up coins from left side and put into left hand, which is then closed tightly again.

5

Pick up coin 5 from right side and palm it. Now pick up coin 6 in fingers.

6

Lay out coins from each hand, retaining coin 5 palmed in right.

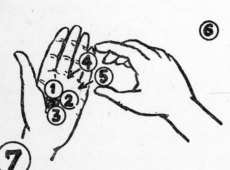

7

Again pick up coins at left and throw one at a time into left hand, secretly adding the palmed coin (No. 5).

8

In picking up coin 6 from right with right hand, secretly slide it off table edge into your lap. Close right hand as though it held this coin.

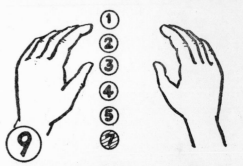

9

Lay out all coins from left hand.

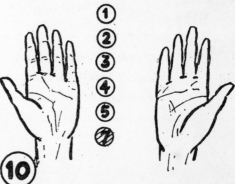

10

Now turn both hands over casually. The three coins from the right side have passed to the left invisibly and you have no spare coins left in either hand!

BANK BALANCE —

1 Your friend places a few pennies on a plate and counts them aloud (ninepence, let's say, in this case)

2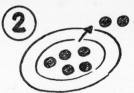

He then "spends" some of the pennies (say 4d) by dropping them in a small envelope ("The Shop") which is then sealed up

3 The remainder are poured into a large envelope ("The Bank") which is sealed firmly and guarded by a member of the audience

4

The small envelope is placed on the plate and is burnt. The four "spent" pennies have vanished!

5 The person guarding the "Bank" then tears open the large envelope and tips the coins out. The original sum (9d) is there, plus an extra penny — interest!

Or — HOW TO SPEND YOUR MONEY — AND YET KEEP IT!

SECRET

(Plate in section)

Use a soup plate with a deep rim on the under-side

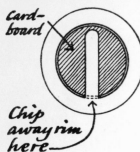

Card-board

Chip away rim here

Fill in the cavity inside the rim with cardboard, leaving a channel big enough to hold five pennies

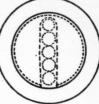

Glue a piece of shiny white card over the rim to hide the five pennies in the channel.

BANK

When the pennies on the plate are tipped into the envelope, the secretly concealed coins go with them.

And where do the "spent" pennies go?

SHOP

The small envelope has a slit in the corner. This is covered by the fingers.

The coins are allowed to slide out into the hand while the big envelope is being sealed. Attention is directed to the big envelope while the magician is "stealing" the "spent" pennies!

And by burning the small envelope, all the evidence of the "crime" is destroyed!

The Melting Coin

"I don't know where my money goes! It just seems to melt away!" you'll hear people say. Show them this quick trick, and they'll really believe that money melts away!

① A spectator holds a coin covered by a handkerchief and drops it into a glass of water held on his other hand.

② 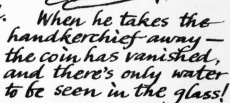 When he takes the handkerchief away — the coin has vanished, and there's only water to be seen in the glass!

SECRET!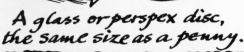
A glass or perspex disc, the same size as a penny.

③ When you place the real coin under the handkerchief, you secretly change it for the glass disc. It is the disc which the spectator drops into the water, and because it's transparent, it's invisible in the water

④ Glass disc lies on left hand and is concealed by the handkerchief.

⑤ Right hand places the coin under handkerchief & drops it in left palm, picking up the glass disc and pushing this towards spectator. When he grasps the disc through handkerchief, your left hand closes on coin and carries it away to pocket.

41

CASH—WITH CARE

Use this vanish of a coin in tricks where you later find the coin in an unusual place!

But although it's been so carefully wrapped up, the coin vanishes from the paper package.

(1) The coin goes into this folded square of paper

(2) The sides of the folded paper are now folded behind to make a packet which is open at the top

(3) The top of the packet is folded back over the other folds. Packet is still open at top. Press round coin to make impression stand out boldly

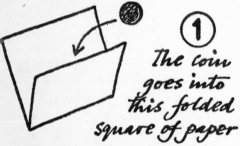

Impression of coin

(4) Packet is taken in right hand, so that coin falls out of open top into hand, where it is palmed.

Impression of coin

(5) Left hand takes empty packet, leaving coin palmed in right hand. The packet can now be torn up or burnt, and the coin produced from some other place.

INTO THIN AIR!

Well—where _does_ the coin go?

A spectator puts a coin into this matchbox:—

He hears it rattle inside the box, but—

When the box is opened, the coin has gone!

SECRET
Prepare the box like this

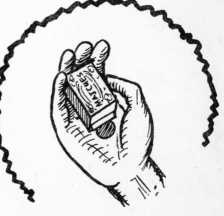

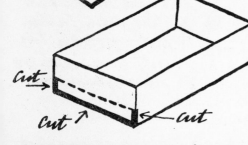

Cut

Cut

Cut

Cut with a razor blade as shown by the heavy lines, and score lightly inside the box along the dotted line. Bend the flap you thus make so that it opens & closes easily.

When you have shaken the box and rattled the coin well, let the coin slide out into your hand through the flap. The blue paper covering the box should act like a spring to close the flap when the coin is out.

OUT OF THIN AIR!

Having caused a coin to vanish, you can just as easily make it reappear inside three boxes (bound together with rubber bands) which you take from your pocket.

Large match box.　Smaller match box.　Smallest match box.

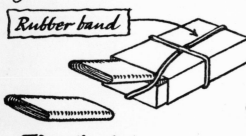

Flat tin tube, small enough to go into smallest match box.

This is placed in next largest box, which in turn goes into biggest box. A rubber band is snapped once each way round each box.

The banded boxes, with tube projecting, are placed in the pocket. The vanished coin (which is palmed) is dropped down the flat funnel, which is then withdrawn & left in the pocket. The rubber bands will close the boxes tightly when the tube is withdrawn

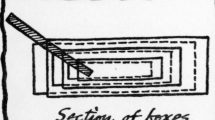

Section of boxes, showing flat tin tube leading to smallest box

Penny in the Bun

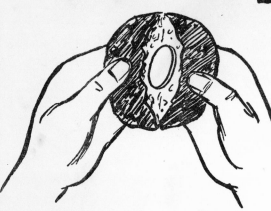

A profitable game, this magic, when you can break open a bun and find a coin inside it!

① The coin is first finger-palmed in the right hand, which holds the bun.

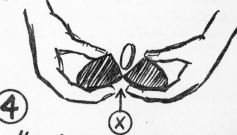

coin

② Hands bend bun _up_ first, making break underneath.

③ Right fingers slip coin in break

④ Hands now bend bun _down_, and up pops the coin!

Ⓧ

IMPORTANT!
Keep the lower halves of the bun Ⓧ together in move ④

The Bank Note Machine

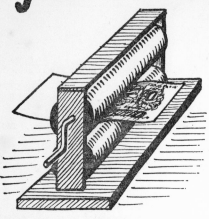

When a blank piece of paper is put between the rollers, it comes out the other side printed like a £1 note!

A black cloth "blind" goes twice round top roller and is then run twice round lower roller in opposite direction.

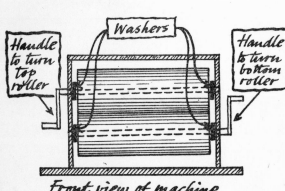

Washers

Handle to turn top roller

Handle to turn bottom roller

Front view of machine

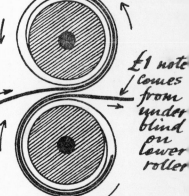

£1 note comes from under blind on lower roller

Blank slip goes under blind on top roller

Enlarged end view of rollers, showing the "blind" that goes round each roller.

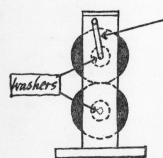

Handle for top roller

Washers

Side view

The £1 note is rolled on to bottom roller before you start the trick.

The SECRETS of PALMING

Learn to palm a coin — it's easy!

1 *The normal palm.*
Coin is gripped
between ball of
thumb & fleshy
edge of hand

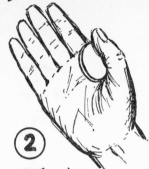

2 *Thumb clip.*
Coin is gripped by
its edge between
thumb & hand

3 *Finger clip.*
As thumb palm,
but between
fingers

4 *Finger palm* Ⓐ.
Coin rests in an
easy position on
the second and
third fingers, &
hand is held in
a natural position

5 *Finger palm* Ⓑ.
Coin is gripped
on lower joints
of second and
third fingers

6 *Back palm.*
Coin is gripped
flat between first
& fourth fingers

IMPORTANT! *Always*
keep the hand relaxed
& easy when palming!

— and card palming isn't difficult, either!

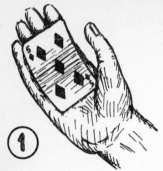

(1)

Contrary to popular belief you don't have to have large hands to palm a card.

This is the regular palm. The card is placed with one corner against the fleshy base of the thumb, and the fingers, slightly curved, press against the other end of the card.

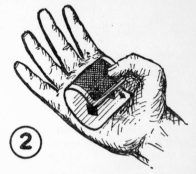

(2)

Using this method, the fingers can be opened wide.

(3)

The back palm. Top corners of card are clipped between fingers at X and X

(4)

Palming a card from the top of the pack. The right hand covers the pack in squaring it up. At the same time, left thumb pushes top card into right palm.

REMEMBER THESE CARD MAGIC TERMS

They'll make it easier to understand the instructions for all card tricks!

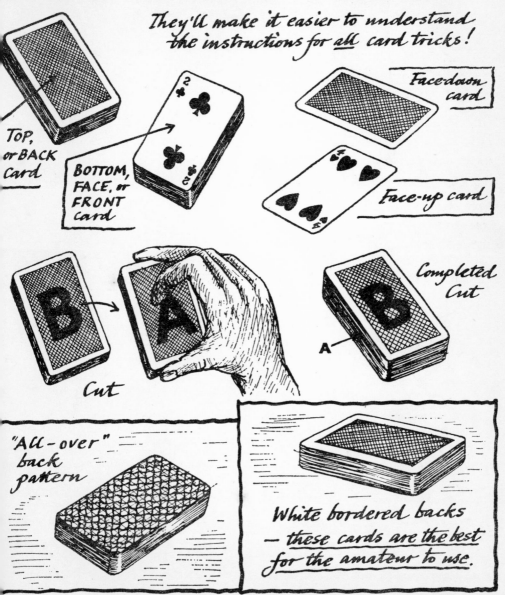

Top, or BACK card

BOTTOM, FACE, or FRONT card

Face-down card

Face-up card

Cut

Completed Cut

A

"All-over" back pattern

White bordered backs — these cards are the best for the amateur to use.

THE FALSE SHUFFLE

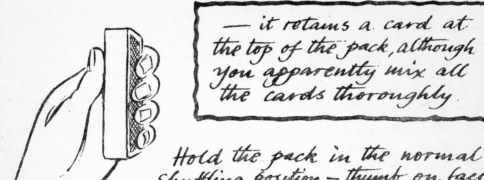

— it retains a card at the top of the pack, although you apparently mix all the cards thoroughly.

Hold the pack in the normal shuffling position — thumb on face card, fingers on back card. Press with fingers on back card

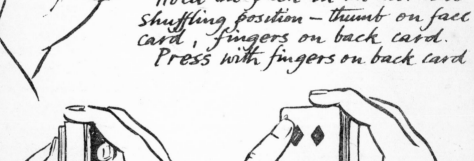

Right hand draws out a portion of cards, but left hand fingers retain the back card (shown shaded)

Right hand drops its cards in front of those retained in left hand. The left hand fingers, pressing against back card, always keep it in the same place.

50

CARD CONTROL

(1)

Many card tricks depend upon cards being controlled and brought to a certain position in the pack — say, to the top or the bottom from the middle of the pack

Learn to hold the cards in this left-hand grip. Note how all four corners of the pack are firmly controlled by the thumb, base of thumb, forefinger and little finger.

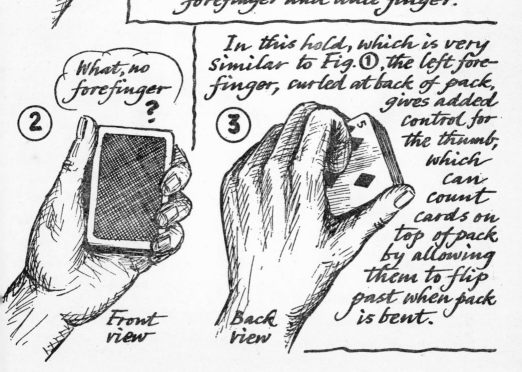

(2) *What, no forefinger?*

Front view

(3)

In this hold, which is very similar to Fig.①, the left fore-finger, curled at back of pack, gives added control for the thumb, which can count cards on top of pack by allowing them to flip past when pack is bent.

Back view

To control a card to the top of the pack

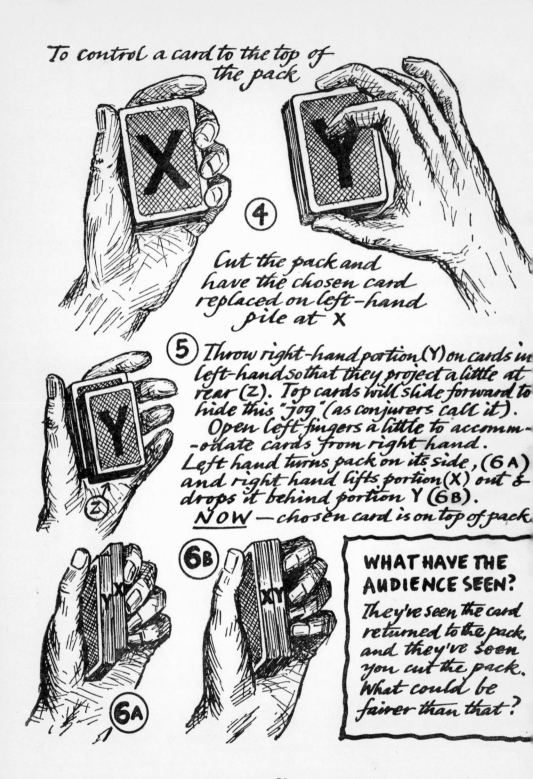

④ Cut the pack and have the chosen card replaced on left-hand pile at X

⑤ Throw right-hand portion (Y) on cards in left-hand so that they project a little at rear (Z). Top cards will slide forward to hide this "jog" (as conjurers call it).
Open left fingers a little to accommodate cards from right hand.
Left hand turns pack on its side, (6A) and right hand lifts portion (X) out & drops it behind portion Y (6B).
<u>N O W</u> — chosen card is on top of pack.

WHAT HAVE THE AUDIENCE SEEN?
They've seen the card returned to the pack, and they've seen you cut the pack. What could be fairer than that?

52

X MARKS THE SPOT!

Have the card you wish to force, on top of the pack

"Force" card

You may need to "force" a card on a spectator. Here's the way to do it without using sleight of hand. It's known as "X-ing the cut"

Invite the spectator to cut the pack & place the lower half _across_ the upper half — "so that you can see just where you cut!"

"Force" card

A — Upper half   B — Lower half

"Force" card

A →   ← B

"Force" card

B ↑   A →

Now you must distract his attention for a few moments, so that he _forgets_ which half of the pack is which — and you'll be amazed how easy it is to confuse a spectator who has "X-ed the cut"!

When you've engaged him in conversation for a few seconds, have him lift off the top packet of cards — "where you cut!" — and look at the top card of the lower packet —

He'll be looking at the card which was originally on top of the pack — the card you've "forced" on him!

Another CARD FORCE

Not infallible — but is a subtle way to make a person take the card you wish him to take.

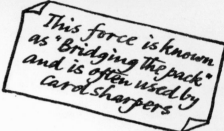
This force is known as "Bridging the pack" and is often used by card sharpers

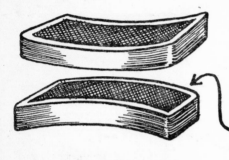

Divide the pack in halves. Bend each half in opposite directions. The "force" card is on top of the lower half

Gap is exaggerated here, for clarity

If you hold the pack by the _sides_, your spectator will cut at the _ends_, where the gap is, and will then, at your invitation, take the top card of the lower heap, and that, of course, is the card you've looked at beforehand!

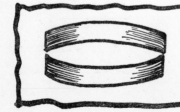

Try bending the cards this way, too.

THE GLIDE

An important card sleight which is used in many tricks. In this one, you produce the Ace of Spades at any position in the pack.

When the audience have named a number, you count out cards and find the Ace at that number.

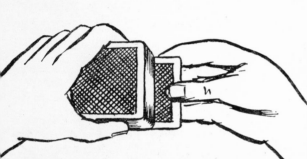

Cards are drawn one at a time from the bottom of the pack BUT — look at this underneath view ↘

SECRET

The Ace is already on the bottom of pack

The left little finger draws back the ace, so that right fingers can take the card above it each time — until you come to the number the audience have named.

2 OUT OF 52

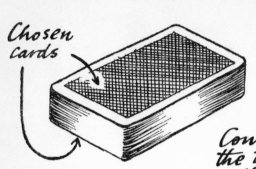

Chosen cards

In which you catch two chosen cards when the pack is thrown into the air

Control one chosen card to the top of the pack and the other to the bottom.

The thumb and fingers of the right hand are moistened secretly. Pack is gripped like this, with pressure applied by thumb & fingers.

Stand with left side to audience. Throw pack in the air, & bring arm quickly to side as shown by dotted line.

Top and bottom cards stay in hand, thanks to wet fingers & thumb.

As the cards are falling, dart right hand into shower and reveal the two cards quickly

THE TURNOVER CARD

FIRST METHOD

After having secretly brought the chosen card to the top of the pack, push it forward half an inch and hold the pack by the sides in the right hand.

This is what happens when you allow the pack to fall to the ground ——————

① Projecting card is caught by up-rush of air and starts to turn over as pack falls.

② Card is here shown turning over.

③ Pack has nearly reached the floor; chosen card is almost reversed.

④ Pack hits floor and chosen card settles down, face-up, on the scattered face-down cards ——————

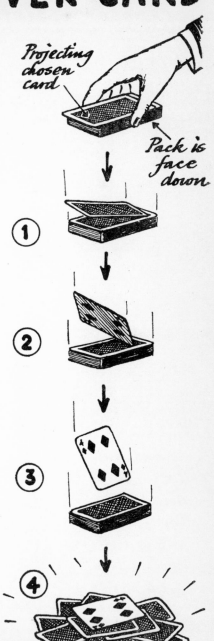

Projecting chosen card

Pack is face down

① ② ③ ④

57

Here are two methods of making a chosen card turn over in the pack, so that it's the only reversed card out of the 52.

In each method you must first "control" the card to the top of the pack

SECOND METHOD

This time, the chosen card has been brought to top of pack & has been pushed __sideways__ half an inch

The pack is deftly thrown along table top so that it spreads out in a ribbon of cards.

Again, the rush of air catches the projecting card and turns it over, at the same time lifting it up.

chosen card

The pack shoots forward and the turned-over card settles down in the middle of the spread, face-up on top of the face-down cards.

THE FAMOUS 4-ACE TRICK

The audience see you — or think they see you! — deal four face-down piles of cards, each containing an ace. But when you turn over the cards, all the aces have collected themselves together in one pile!

FIRST — *THE SECRET!*

3 ordinary cards (*not* aces) are hidden, face-down, under the card case.

① Have a spectator sort out the aces from the pack.

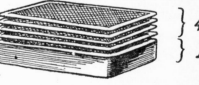

② After he's mixed them up, tell him to lay them, face-down, on top of the pack.

} 4 aces
} Pack

③ Pick up the card case, carefully retaining the 3 hidden cards beneath it, and lay it on top of the pack. This adds 3 cards on top of the aces.

Ⓐ

3 cards
4 aces
Rest of pack

Ⓑ

CONJURERS SAY THERE ARE HUNDREDS OF METHODS OF PERFORMING THIS TRICK. HERE'S ONE OF THE SIMPLEST!

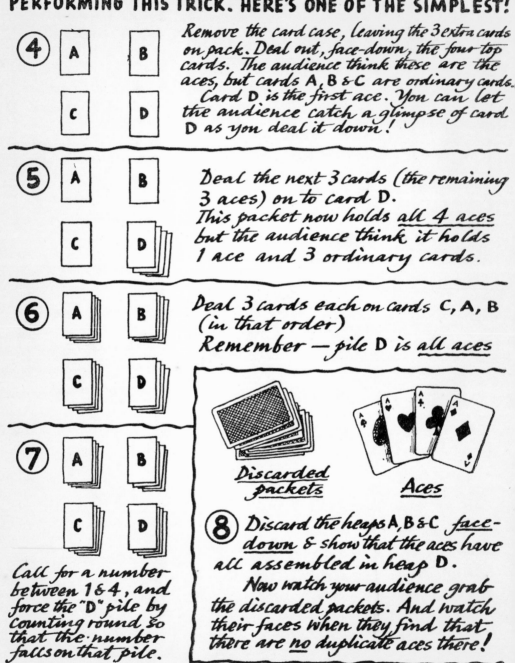

(4) A B C D

Remove the card case, leaving the 3 extra cards on pack. Deal out, face-down, the four top cards. The audience think these are the aces, but cards A, B & C are ordinary cards.
Card D is the first ace. You can let the audience catch a glimpse of card D as you deal it down!

(5) A B C D

Deal the next 3 cards (the remaining 3 aces) on to card D.
This packet now holds all 4 aces but the audience think it holds 1 ace and 3 ordinary cards.

(6) A B C D

Deal 3 cards each on cards C, A, B (in that order)
Remember — pile D is all aces

Discarded packets   Aces

(7) A B C D

Call for a number between 1 & 4, and force the "D" pile by counting round so that the number falls on that pile.

(8) Discard the heaps A, B & C face-down & show that the aces have all assembled in heap D.
Now watch your audience grab the discarded packets. And watch their faces when they find that there are no duplicate aces there!

60

THE MARVELLOUS STRIPPER PACK!

The stripper pack has one end slightly narrower than the other end — but no more than $\frac{1}{16}$"

This pack is sometimes known as "The Wizard's Pack", or "The BISEAUTÉ Pack". You can buy it at a Magic Shop, or have it prepared for you by your local printer, who has a machine that will cut the cards accurately.

When a card is replaced with its wide end among the narrower ends, it can be felt by the projection of its wide end.

So if you turn the pack round after a card has been chosen and then have the selected card replaced, it will be reversed and can be found easily.

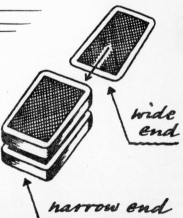

wide end

narrow end

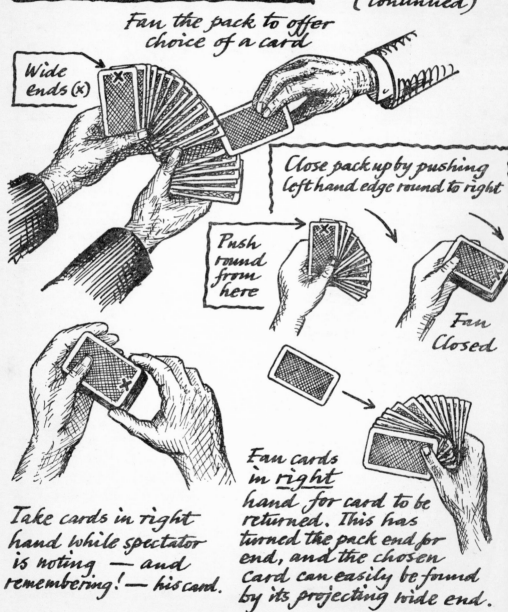

Use <u>technique</u> in turning the pack round for the chosen card to be returned!

THE MARVELLOUS STRIPPER PACK
(continued)

Fan the pack to offer choice of a card

Wide ends (x)

Close pack up by pushing left hand edge round to right

Push round from here

Fan Closed

Fan cards in <u>right</u> hand for card to be returned. This has turned the pack end for end, and the chosen card can easily be found by its projecting wide end.

Take cards in right hand while spectator is noting — and remembering! — his card.

The World's Longest Trick!

After a spectator has chosen a card & replaced it in the pack, you turn your back for a moment. "I'm going to find your card & put it in my pocket," you tell him. Now turn round and face him again....

Is this your card?

You then draw a card part-way out of your breast pocket.

NO!

But when you take the same card out of your pocket he will admit that the suit and the number of pips _do_ match the card he took!

Fingers cover corner where index pips would be

You'll have to make a slit in the bottom of your breast pocket to accommodate this long, long card.

P.S. You forced the 10 of Diamonds on him by — "X-ing the cut"!

"And I shuffled the Cards myself!"

That's what the amazed spectator will say when he sees you do this trick!

A shuffled pack of cards is placed back in its box by a spectator — but without touching either the box or the cards you can tell him the order the cards are in!

8 of Spades!
2 of Clubs!
Queen of Hearts!
9 of Diamonds!

Don't draw attention to the box! It holds the —

SECRET!

Closed End

Make yourself a card box like this! It's like a big match-box with a loosely fitting tray and with one end closed.

memorized loose cards

Pack of Cards

Before you start the trick, take half a dozen or so cards, _memorize_ them, and slip them between tray & box. Have the box open on your table. Have the pack shuffled and placed in the box, and tell the spectator to close the box. The loose cards secretly placed between tray and box will fall into the tray, _on top_ of his shuffled cards when he closes the box. You can now name them and have him check the pack.

SOMETHING UP YOUR SLEEVE!

A ghostly bit of business, in which the name of a chosen card appears, in letters of black or red, on the conjurer's arm!

First, arrange to "force" your card on the spectator, as explained in "X MARKS THE SPOT"

If you want to force a black card, you'll have to make _this_ preparation beforehand—

If you prefer a _red card_

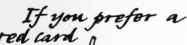

Write the name of the card on your left arm with a piece of soap (it won't show!)

draw the pips on the flesh with a blunt stick. —— The red impression will soon fade. When you're ready to perform the trick, pull up your sleeve —

Have the name of the card (after it's been chosen) written on a piece of paper & burnt. Rub the ashes of the paper on your arm and—

4 OF SPADES

rub your arm vigorously, and the red marks spring to life brightly again!

the black ashes stick to the soaped letters.

THE BOOMERANG

HERE'S WHAT HAPPENS :—

A card is chosen & remembered by a spectator, who returns it to the pack and cuts the pack. The conjurer takes the Joker, flips it through the air like a boomerang, and when it returns to him he catches it in the pack like this —

He lifts the Joker, thus raising the top half of the pack. The card beneath the Joker is turned over, and is found to be — the chosen card!

Joker

chosen card

SECRET!

In this trick we make use of a "locator" card. This time it's a card slightly _wider_ than the rest of the pack. Being wider, it projects at the side and can easily be found by touch.

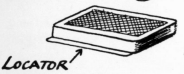

LOCATOR

Cut the pack at the wide card, and complete the cut, so that the wide "locator" is at bottom of pack.

Have chosen card replaced on top of pack

Now let the spectator cut the pack and complete the cut. This puts the chosen card in middle of pack _with the wide locator immediately above it_

CARD

The Boomerang card trick once depended upon an intricate piece of sleight of hand. Here is a simple way of performing this spectacular trick.

The pack is taken in the left hand & the Joker is spun through the air by the right hand. Joker is gripped between first two fingers and sent spinning forward. **PRACTISE THIS WELL!**

With practise you will be able to make the card return like a boomerang, and catch it in the pack held in the left hand.

Left hand holds pack on its side, with thumb on edge of the wide card, ready to catch Joker

Joker is caught here →

Let all cards below wide card fall forward on to outstretched fingers.

Chosen card will be here

When Joker is caught between "jaws" of pack, snap the pack shut again quickly.

Have a spectator lift the cards above the Joker and find the chosen card immediately below it.

The opening and closing of the pack must be covered by a wide sweep of the arm, as the left hand brings the open pack forward to meet and catch the spinning Joker.

THE CARD ON THE WALL

Try this one next time you're at a party. Your audience will be amused — and amazed! — when they see you throw the pack at the wall. They'll be even more amazed when the chosen card is seen _sticking to the wall_, after the other cards have fallen to the ground!

Here's the chosen card

② Have the card chosen, looked at, remembered, and replaced in the pack. Control it to the top of the pack.

SECRET

sticky side

— A band of cellulose adhesive tape ("Scotch tape") just big enough to fit loosely on the end of a finger. The sticky side is outward.

③ Place pack in left hand pressing back card (the chosen one) on sticky band. When you remove the pack, do so with a sliding motion, so that sticky band is slid off finger end & sticks to back card ⟶

① Keep the finger with the sticky band on it folded into the palm.

④ Throw pack squarely at a high point on wall. The back card must hit the wall first and it will stick firmly, while the rest of the pack falls.

THE CARD THROUGH THE TABLE

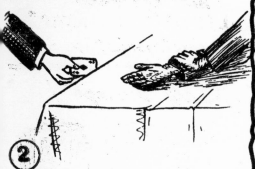

When you've had a card chosen and looked at by your audience — and then returned to the pack — control it to the top, and —

1 Invite the chooser of the card to press the back of his hand on the pack, which is face-down on the table. Show him just how to do it — as in the sketch above.

SECRET!

2 When he has pressed the cards really hard — you reach under the table, and bring out the chosen card!

Watch the angles!

3 Secretly lick the back of your hand before you press the back of the cards. The top (chosen) card will be carried away on the back of your hand, which you place under the table ready for the grand finale!

FIVE CHOICES

Before this trick is shown, you lay a sealed envelope on the table. When the trick is over, the envelope is opened, and it is found that you have successfully predicted which cards a spectator would choose!

On the table are your sealed envelope and five heaps of cards, face down. A spectator is invited to choose any heap. He turns over his cards, opens the envelope and reads aloud the message it contains.

The message reads:—
"YOU WILL CHOOSE THE 5 HEAP"
and that's exactly what he's done!

SECRET—

He could have chosen any of the other heaps, and he'd still have chosen "The 5 Heap."

Because — They're all "5 Heaps"!

5 ← (1) →	4 (2)	3 (3)	2 (4)	← 1 (→ 5)
This heap (any number of cards *more than 5*) is *No. 5* from the right-hand end of row.	In this heap the pips total *5*	This heap contains the four *5 s*	This heap has *5* Cards in it	This heap (any number of cards *more* than 5) is *No. 5* from the left-hand end of row.

The Card with **FOUR** Sides !

It's impossible, of course for a card to have FOUR sides, but—

① *You can show that one side bears an <u>ace</u>,*

② *this side has <u>four spots</u>,*

③ *this side has <u>three</u>,*

④ *and this side has <u>six spots</u>.*

These sketches, though, show that the

SECRET ➡️

is an easy one !

The fingers, as shown in the drawings 1, 2, 3 & 4, cover blank spaces or spots as required.

Practise well in front of a mirror, and especially watch the way you change the card from hand to hand and turn it round !

 *hand covers spot*

 *hand covers spot*

 *hand covers space*

 hand covers space

STRONG MAN STUFF!

It needs great strength indeed to tear a pack of cards in half.

Here are some easy ways to do it.

The easiest — bake the cards in a hot oven. They become brittle and easy to tear.

Make a one inch cut through the edge of the pack. Hide this by a loose card on top and bottom.

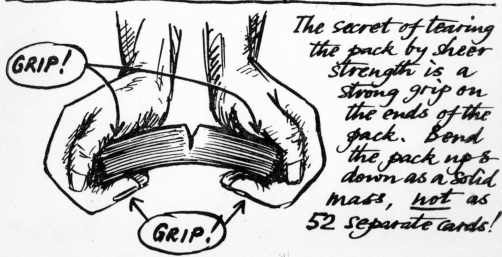

GRIP!

GRIP!

The secret of tearing the pack by sheer strength is a strong grip on the ends of the pack. Bend the pack up & down as a solid mass, not as 52 separate cards!

THE ROMANS HAD A WORD FOR IT!

An old, old trick, but one that's still popular.

① Ten pairs of cards are laid face-down. Ten people are invited to look at and remember a pair each.

First Row

Second Row

Third Row

Fourth Row

② The pairs are gathered up _face down_, and are then dealt out _face up_ in four rows.

The audience are then asked to point to the rows in which are the cards they looked at. As each person points to a row, you are able to name his cards.

HERE'S HOW ➚

SECRET

The secret is in the way the cards are laid out when you deal them into the four rows.

You must memorise this sentence — **DAVID LOVEL IN YON ABBEY**. It contains 10 pairs of letters. The cards are dealt on to the places the letters would occupy if they were written on the table like this —

1	2	3	4	1
5	6	3	7	5
4	8	9	6	8
2	10	10	7	9

The pairs are laid out in this order, to coincide with the paired letters in the sentence

The first pair of cards goes on the two Ds in "DaviD". The next pair goes on the two As (Rows 1 & 4). The third pair of cards goes on the two Vs (Rows 1 & 2) and so on till all the cards are dealt out.

(Row 1) — **D A V I D**
(Row 2) — **L O V E L**
(Row 3) — **I N Y O N**
(Row 4) — **A B B E Y**

When your audience point to the rows in which they see their cards, you think of the pair of letters in those rows, and are thus able to identify the cards on those letters.

Here's another formula for the same trick. It is said to date back to Roman times, & uses the Latin words

M U T U S
N O M E N
C O C I S
D E D I T

(which mean "Mutus gave a name to Cocis")

74

JUMPING COLOURS

A red rubber band on 1st. & 2nd. fingers, a green rubber band on 3rd. & 4th. fingers.	Close the fist—	and when you open your hand again, the rubber bands have changed places !

(1) Let bands slip to lower joints

(2) Right forefinger & thumb take band Ⓑ

(3) Right forefinger brings band Ⓑ over band Ⓐ

(4) Right forefinger hooks into band Ⓐ

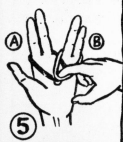

(5) Right finger stretches bands downwards

(6) Right second finger opens out crossed bands

(7) Fingers are folded down into ⊗ —(Fig 6). Right hand moves away

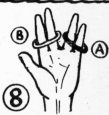

(8) Open hand out smartly, & the bands appear to leap across & change places.

The Magic Circlet

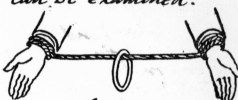

A large slave bangle passes on to a rope tied round both wrists. Both rope & bangle are free from trickery and can be examined.

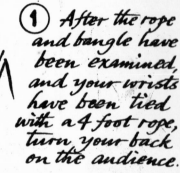

SECRET

There are <u>two</u> bangles. One is on your arm inside your sleeve before you start the trick

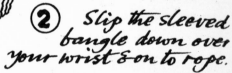

① After the rope and bangle have been examined, and your wrists have been tied with a 4 foot rope, turn your back on the audience.

② Slip the sleeved bangle down over your wrist & on to rope.

③ Place the examined bangle in your inside coat pocket.

④ Turn back to the audience — and let them puzzle out how the bangle got on the rope.

Bangle from sleeve

Examined bangle goes in pocket

THE OBEDIENT ORANGE

Thread it on a cord, run it up and down to show that it runs freely, and say—

STOP!

The orange will stop dead. *Why?*

Here's the

SECRET—

It's a thin, bent metal funnel, which is secretly inserted into the orange when piercing the hole.

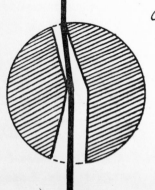

The kink in the middle of the tube stops the orange falling when the cord is tightened.

The Cube & Frame

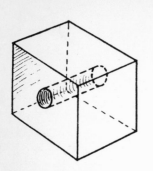

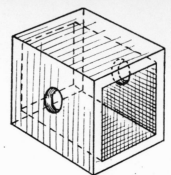

A wooden cube with a 1 inch hole drilled through it —

A wooden frame to fit the cube loosely, with corresponding holes —

6 feet of ribbon.

THESE MAKE A MIRACLE!

Although the audience hold the ribbon, which is threaded through cube and frame,

The magician is able to take the cube out of the frame and off the ribbon.

SECRET ➤➤➤

A reel of thread and

several dabs of beeswax

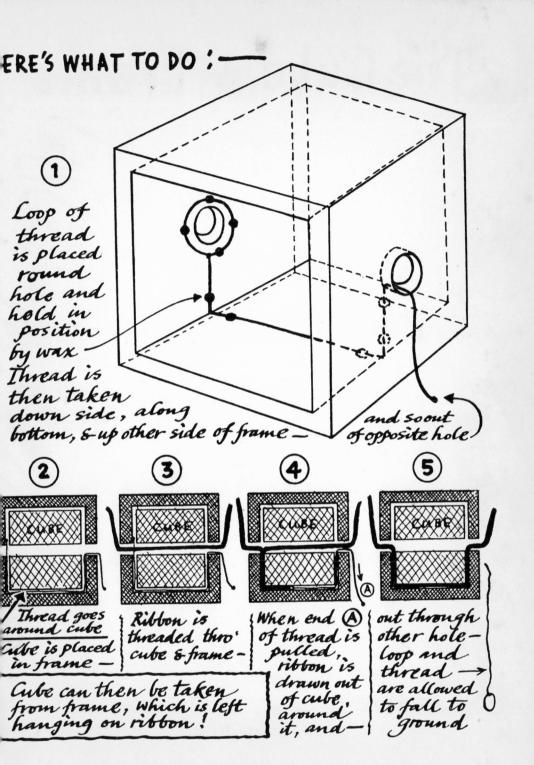

ERE'S WHAT TO DO :—

1

Loop of thread is placed round hole and held in position by wax — Thread is then taken down side, along bottom, & up other side of frame —

and so out of opposite hole

2

Thread goes around cube — Cube is placed in frame —

3

Ribbon is threaded thro' cube & frame —

4

When end Ⓐ of thread is pulled, ribbon is drawn out of cube, around it, and—

5

out through other hole — loop and thread → are allowed to fall to ground

Cube can then be taken from frame, which is left hanging on ribbon !

THE SNAP KNOT

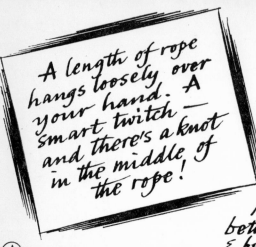

A length of rope hangs loosely over your hand. A smart twitch — and there's a knot in the middle of the rope!

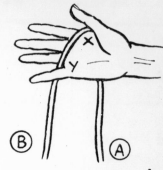

B   A

IMPORTANT!
Note how rope is gripped between thumb & hand at X & between 3rd. & 4th. fingers at Y

1
Hand drops downward quickly, and catches end (A) between first two fingers.

2
Hand turns down, and releases rope, all except end (A)

3
A quick jerk, like cracking a whip, tightens the knot.

A trick with
POLO – The Mint with the Hole!

Next time you buy a packet of Polo mints try this trick ——

(1) Have your friend thread a mint (X) on a string.

(2) Then thread the other mints over the ends of the doubled string. While your friend holds the ends of the string —— (3) place a handkerchief over the mints.

(4) Then comes the climax! Pop your hands under the handkerchief, and **POLO**! the mints fall off the string — _all except the one that's holding them in place_!

THIS TIME THERE ARE **2 SECRETS**!

(A) The last mint (z) isn't threaded on the doubled string. It goes on _one string_ only. This is the mint that stays on the string when —

(B) you _break_ mint X and secretly take it away as the other mints fall.

Almost <u>The</u> Indian Rope Trick

A coil of rope — a magic word — and the rope can be stretched out in a rigid length

SECRET (1)

SECRET (2)

The rope is hollow (soft sashcord is ideal)

A piece of soft copper wire is threaded into the rope —

Copper wire →

ROPE

for half its length. The rope can still be coiled, even with the wire in it.

Now, uncoil rope and —

SECRET (3)

Even better than soft copper wire is "MULTICORE SOLDER." It's softer, but stronger and more rigid than copper wire

Pull hands
← apart →

shaded portion has wire inside rope

One hand holds rope at middle. Wired half of rope is allowed to project in a straight line. Other hand stretches unprepared half of rope to keep it taut.

The INDESTRUCTIBLE ROPE!

Most "cut & restored" rope tricks are done by means of a trick loop of rope. Here's one that's different!

1 Rope is threaded through a hole pierced in a block of wood 15" x 1½" x 1½"

cut

2 The block, which is hinged at the middle, is opened at the hinge, and the loop of rope is cut where it protrudes. Block is then closed, and rope pulled out whole!

Hole through which rope is threaded

Secret hole contains duplicate piece of rope

3 Side view of wooden block shows secret hole with duplicate piece of rope

4 View of underside of block, showing cut-out portion (shaded) between hinges

5 Close-up of block of wood folded, showing genuine rope drawn down and duplicate piece ready to cut.

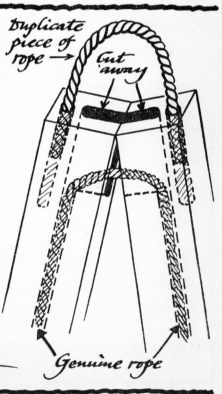

Duplicate piece of rope →

Cut away

Genuine rope

GOING UP!

A magazine, two pieces of string, two paper clips — these make a mystery in which the rolled magazine rides up and down the strings as you hold them!

The
SECRET

lies in the way you thread the strings through the tube made by the rolled magazine →

Here's a sectioned view of the tube. Instead of the strings running right through side by side, String Ⓐ (dark) is hooked on the lower paper-clip. String Ⓑ (light) is looped round string Ⓐ.

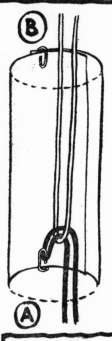

These sketches show light & dark strings for clearness. — But your strings should both be light

Start with the magazine at its lowest point, when strings will be as shown here

When strings Ⓐ are tightened, the tube rises, and strings will be in this position at tube's highest point

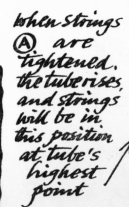

84

THROUGH THE TUNNEL

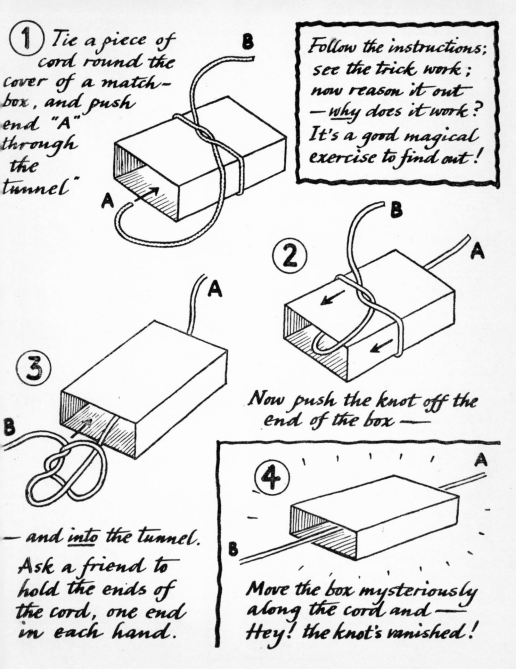

1 Tie a piece of cord round the cover of a match-box, and push end "A" through the tunnel"

Follow the instructions; see the trick work; now reason it out — *why* does it work? It's a good magical exercise to find out!

B

A

2

B

A

Now push the knot off the end of the box —

3

B

— and *into* the tunnel. Ask a friend to hold the ends of the cord, one end in each hand.

4

A

B

Move the box mysteriously along the cord and — Hey! the knot's vanished!

THE STRING & THE STRAW

Thread a string through a straw; cut the straw through the middle — what happens? You've cut the string! But not if you do it this way —

cut

SECRET

TO PERFORM —

Cut a fine slit, one inch long, in one side of the straw at the middle. Use a razor blade to get a fine cut.

(1) Thread the string through the straw

(2) Bend the straw at the middle (Slit is shown thicker in the sketch)

(3) Pull down the ends of the string so that the middle is drawn down the slit at Ⓧ Now push the point of the scissors in *above* the middle of the string and — *CUT!*

(4) Draw the halves of the straw apart and show that the string is undamaged

This Reef Knot is a Slip-knot!

This is a reef knot — left over right and right over left. It's generally believed to be a firm, solid knot. So it is — until you upset it like this :—

Here's an interesting and baffling feat that can be performed with ropes, tapes, string or handkerchieves. It's a useful principle — practise well !

①

Pull the knot _tight_ — as tight as you like. Let your audience check that it's good & tight.

②

[A] [B]

Under pretence of pulling the knot _more_ tight, pull firmly on one rope at [A] and [B]

③

You will now find that the other rope will slide easily off the end [B]

Always cover the upset knot in the fist

By clenching the fist, you can have your audience tug strongly on the ropes. When you relax your grip, the ropes part in a flash!

The KNOT THAT'S NOT!

TOP SECRET CENSORED!

A knot in a piece of rope — a magic word —

and the knot's NOT!

HERE'S HOW —

A ●————————————● B

① *Shaded spots indicate spots of "Copydex" latex cement applied to rope.*

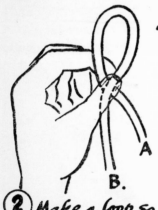

② *Make a loop so that the two spots of cement join together. Note the end "B" of rope is in front of end "A"*

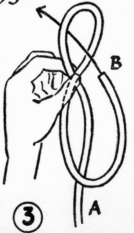

③ *Thread end "B" through loop.*

Copydex cement between ropes

A ————————— B

④ *It looks like a knot but — it's not! Pull the ends of the rope — and the spots of Copydex are pulled apart and the "knot" has gone!*

A HOUDINI ESCAPE

Harry Houdini was the greatest expert in escaping from handcuffs, ropes, chains and strait-jackets.
Later, Murray (who coined the word "escapologist") took up Houdini's role & earned great fame escaping from handcuffs, chains, ropes, strait-jackets, locked boxes, and other sensational restraints.

In this escape, the magician releases himself from the rope threaded between his tied wrists. A spectator holds the ends of the rope tightly. A handkerchief has been tied round the performer's wrists previously.

① Rope is manipulated between "heels" of hands —

② —and up towards knuckles.

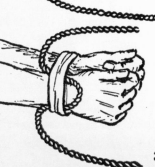

③ One hand is slipped through the loop when it reaches the knuckles —

④ Then a brisk tug, and the rope slips through the handkerchief at ⊗ – ⊗

THE GREAT SACK ESCAPE!

Here's the way to escape from a sack after the mouth of the sack has been roped and sealed by your audience

① You'll need two sacks made of thin black material. One is hidden under your coat when you climb into the other sack

② When the mouth of the sack is being bunched up above your heads they're ready to tie it up —

③ — push the mouth of your duplicate sack up through the fist of your assistant (who is in the secret).

Duplicate Sack

First Sack

He wraps one *turn* of rope round the genuine sack, and the rest round the duplicate sack. You can thus pull the first sack away from the rope, which is left tied round the duplicate sack mouth.

Your escape is made behind a screen. When you are out of the original sack, hide it under your coat and bring forward the duplicate sack, which now has the knotted & sealed rope round it.

ROBIN HOOD escapes again

Although Robin Hood's picture has been firmly rivetted (by a large paper clip) inside the model of a cell, it escapes as easily as the hero of Sherwood Forest escaped from the dungeons of Nottingham Castle.

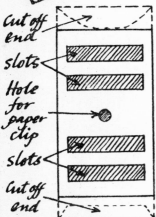

Cut off end

slots

Hole for paper clip

slots

Cut off end

The "dungeon" is a long envelope with the ends cut off, and wide slots cut through to represent bars.

Hole for paper clip

The picture of Robin Hood is on thin card, long enough to project at each end of the "dungeon."

<u>N.B.</u> It's <u>width is a little narrower than the slots in the envelope.</u>

SECRET

Paper clip head is smaller than hole in card

<u>Back View</u>

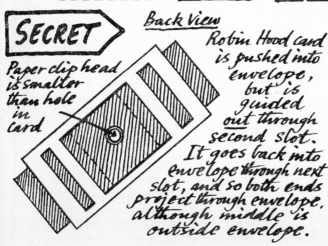

Robin Hood card is pushed into envelope, but is guided out through second slot. It goes back into envelope through next slot, and so both ends project through envelope, although middle is outside envelope.

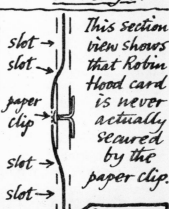

slot →
slot →

paper clip →

slot →
slot →

This section view shows that Robin Hood card is never actually secured by the paper clip.

SECTION

THE ELECTRONIC BRAIN

— couldn't calculate more accurately than the magician who uses these numbered cards! Conjurers know them as 'The Age Cards'

HERE'S HOW!

MAKE YOURSELF A SET OF AGE CARDS & BUILD YOURSELF A REPUTATION AS A MIND-READER!

With the Age Cards, you can tell a person the number he is thinking of. You can tell him how old he is, if he thinks of his own age.. You can tell him the number of his house, if it is between 1 and 100. — With this set of 7 cards, in fact, you can at once divine _any_ number, so long as it's a whole number between 1 and 100

THE SECRET:—

Each card has a "key" number which you must note & remember. It's the number at the top left hand corner of each card. These numbers are 1, 2, 4, 8, 16, 32 & 64. It will help you if you pencil each card's key number lightly on the back of the card. If you wish to mark the key number secretly, use this code of dots:—

Key No.	
(4)	15
5	20
6	21
	22

1 = ⌐

8 = ⎓

2 = ⌐

16 = ⌐

4 = ⌐

32 = ⌐

64 = [•

Ask your friend to think of a number between 1 and 100, and tell him to pick up all cards bearing that number.

You can either note the key numbers from the front as he picks up the cards, or else note them from the marks you have made on the backs of the cards.

To tell him his number, simply _add the key numbers of the cards_ he has picked up.

EXAMPLE :-

He holds cards bearing Key Numbers 1, 16 & 64. He is thinking of the number 81

GHOST IN THE PARLOUR

What makes the table float in the air when you lay your hands flat on it?

GHOSTS?

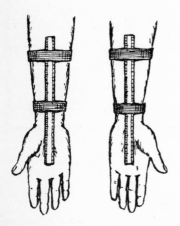

Well — no. HERE'S THE SECRET. It's up the sleeve!

Strap a flat ruler on the under-side of each arm — before you put your coat on, of course!

Lift — and up comes the table But pick on a lightweight table!

Hands on table

Sleeve

Rulers under table

The SPIRITS Tell!

Hand to a spectator a large card like a calendar. Ask him to turn his back & place his finger on the day of the month on which he was born, and to count silently to that number. (The 0 is there for him to use if he doesn't know his birthday!)

Although he does all this secretly, the spirits tell you the date of his birth when he gives the card back to you!

NOTE! Expose the luminous card to the light to "charge" it before you do the trick.

—at least, that's *your* story! Really, the card, painted with LUMINOUS PAINT, tells you the date. The figure on which he placed his finger will be dull, while the rest of the card will glow, as soon as you place the card in shadow.

		1	2	3	4
5	6	7	8	9	10
11	12	13	14	15	16
17	18	19	20	21	22
23	24	25	26	27	28
	29	30	31	0	

The Psychometric Boxes

Six numbered boxes, with hinged lids, and six ping-pong balls, numbered to match the boxes, are used.

A ball is put into each box and the boxes are closed. Then, while you are out of the room, the audience open one box and pass the ball round to each person for examination. The ball is replaced in its box, the lid is closed, and you are brought back into the room. By looking at each box, you can tell "from the vibrations it contains" which ball has been handled by the audience.

SECRET—

— a trick pencil!
It's a propelling pencil with no lead in it, into which you have put some salt.

You close each lid with the pencil — "So as not to impose any personal vibrations on the box". A few grains of salt are deposited on each lid.

When one box is opened, the salt grains on its lid fall on the table. Look for a box behind which are some salt grains, and that's the box they've opened!

Use white boxes (the salt won't show on them) & a dark table (the salt will show on that!)

The Number <u>You</u> Want!

108? 99? 101?
16? **79!** 72?
34? 9?
4? 20? 38?

There may be occasions when you require to "force" a number. Here's a sure way of doing it.

73? 12? 41?
8? **79!** 203?
62? 22?
1008? 11?
3?

Prepare 100 small cards 1" square bearing numbers 1–100

Make a duplicate set of cards, each bearing the same number – the number you wish to force.

Ticket pocket

This hand opens pocket

This hand covers ticket pocket

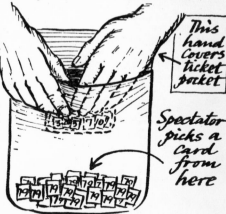

Spectator picks a card from here

The 1–100 cards are placed in the small ticket pocket inside the jacket pocket. The force-numbered cards are at the bottom of the large pocket.

Show the cards 1–100 and put them back in the ticket pocket, "to give a free & uninfluenced" choice

In holding your pocket open so that a spectator may put in his hand and choose a card, your hand covers the ticket pocket. The spectator can only take a "force" card!

A BAFFLING BOOK MYSTERY

Here's a mystifying trick using "A NUMBER YOU WANT." In it, you divine a word chosen by a member of the audience from a book.

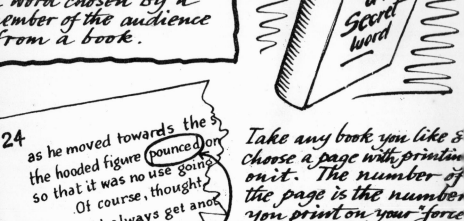

THE MYSTERY OF THE Secret word

24

as he moved towards the s
the hooded figure pounced on
so that it was no use going
Of course, thought
one could always get anot
takes away with him

2nd. line
4th. word

Disclose the word you have "thought-read" as dramatically as you can!

Take any book you like & choose a page with printing on it. The number of the page is the number you print on your "force" cards — in this case 24.

Remember the 4th word of the 2nd. line.

Have the book examined by your audience, and then offer them "a free choice" of any page, by the number force in "A NUMBER YOU WANT."

Invite a spectator to turn to the page he has chosen & to count to the line represented by the first digit of this page number, and the word indicated by the next digit.

THE DICTIONARY TEST

A variation of the book test — for use in case the audience say "Do it again!"

You use a pocket dictionary but **don't** draw attention to it's being a "pocket" dictionary

1 This time you give a pocket dictionary to the audience, who are to choose a page & a word in it, while you are behind the door.
Ask them to call out the page number and the number of the line containing their word.

2 When you return to the room you slowly and mysteriously divine the chosen word.

SECRET — a duplicate dictionary in your pocket! You rapidly turn up the word as they tell you the page number, keep talking and re-enter the room.

The Domino Mystery

While you are out of the room, the audience lay out a set of dominoes on the table, placing matching spots together as in the game of dominoes. They then turn over the dominoes at each end of the row so that they are face down, & so that you can't see them.

But you can still name the pips on the end dominoes although you can't see them!

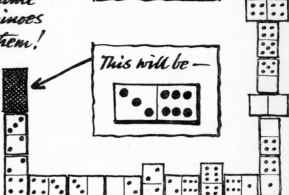

Face—down domino will be—

This will be—

SECRET —

You have secretly popped a domino in your pocket, and thus deprived the audience of the use of it.

The end spots will match those on the domino you have "stolen"

You could make a good strong "prediction" mystery out of this by writing the name of the "stolen" domino in a sealed envelope, which you place on the table before the game is played.

THE SPIRIT WRITES!

When next you're sitting round the fire on a bitter winter's night, with the wind howling in the chimney, make your friends **SHUDDER** with this example of ghost-writing!

When all hands are on the table & the lights are low, hold a slate and chalk under the table and the spirits will write!

And to prove that it's really ghost-writing— they'll have to hold it up to a mirror to read it!

Here's how to do fast "mirror-writing"— Hold the slate firmly against the under-side of the table top, and write on the under-side of slate AS THOUGH YOU WERE TRACING A MESSAGE ALREADY WRITTEN ON A GLASS SLATE

Hand writes below

Imagine the words are written on the <u>top</u> side of the glass, and trace them on the bottom side

MATHEMATICAL MYSTERY

After a member of your audience has done a simple sum, and has secretly rubbed out one figure in the answer (and the rest of the sum) you are able to tell him what that figure was!

NOTICE !
TO GET THE BEST OUT OF THIS MYSTERY USE A LARGE BLACKBOARD SO THAT EVERYONE CAN SEE!

① Invite a spectator to write down any four-figure number — say ———— **7825**

② Now tell him to "scramble" the figures ——— **2857**

③ and subtract the smaller number from the larger ———————
$$\begin{array}{r} 7825 \\ 2857 \\ \hline 4968 \end{array}$$

④ He must now rub out the two lines of the sum and <u>one figure</u> of the total, leaving three figures of the total on the blackboard ————— **49 8**

⑤ You <u>know</u>, as soon as you see the three figures left, what figure he rubbed out, because —

SECRET The answer to such a sum always comes to a multiple of 9.

So all you need do is add the remaining figures ———————
$$\begin{array}{r} 4 \\ 9 \\ 8 \\ \hline 21 \end{array}$$

and subtract your answer from the next highest multiple of 9.
$$\begin{array}{r} 27 \\ 21 \\ \hline 6 \end{array}$$

102

MORE MYSTERIOUS MATHS

① Hand a magazine to a member of your audience, together with a pencil and a slip of paper.

The "Nine Principle" is very useful to magicians. Here's another mystery that makes use of it.

② Ask him to work out a four-figure sum like the last item. This time, though, he is to total the digits in the answer.

$$\text{say} - \quad 4961$$
$$\text{subtract} - \quad \underline{1964}$$
$$\quad \underline{2997}$$

③ He gets, of course, a multiple of 9 — $2+9+9+7 = 27$

④ Now, without asking him what his total is (you know it's a multiple of 9!) tell him to turn to that page in the magazine. Without seeing the page he is looking at you can describe the contents of the page!

⑤ — Because you have memorized (roughly) pages 9, 18, 27, 36 & 45 (It rarely goes higher than this)

⑥ But if you want to make the whole thing much easier, simply memorize **PAGE 9**
In that case, at stage **③** — $2+9+9+7 = 27$
the spectator must total up $2+9+7 = 18$
his digits again until they $2+7 = \underline{\underline{9}}$
come to a single figure —
AND IT'S <u>ALWAYS</u> 9!

THE SIDEREAL PENDULUM

The pendulum nearly always swings correctly to show answers to questions. WHY?

Tie a 12 inch thread to a ring, and hold it as in the sketch, with the elbow resting on the table for steadiness.

The pendulum will swing in a circle when held over a girl's hand, and in a straight line over a boy's hand.

More mysterious than that — anyone can do it! And if you tell a person holding the pendulum that, by touching their head, you can make the pendulum change its swing — it WILL change its swing!

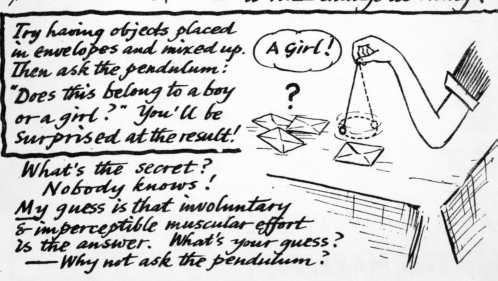

Try having objects placed in envelopes and mixed up. Then ask the pendulum: "Does this belong to a boy or a girl?" You'll be surprised at the result!

A Girl!

?

What's the secret?
    Nobody knows!
My guess is that involuntary & imperceptible muscular effort is the answer. What's your guess?
    — Why not ask the pendulum?

THE MYSTERY OF THE FOUR MARBLES

You are able to distinguish the colours of the marbles without *seeing* them!

Your friend puts the marbles in your hand one at a time, and you turn to him and tell him the colour of each as he gives it to you —

AND YOU NEVER SEE THE MARBLES!

SECRET

A metal ring on a piece of elastic pinned under the back of your coat. One marble goes through the ring *very* easily. Another is a little bigger and is a rather tighter fit. The third is a very tight fit and only goes through the ring with a strong push. The fourth is too big to go through.

The elastic is there to pull the ring back out of sight again after the trick.

EARS at your FINGER TIPS!

To "prove" that there's telepathy between yourself and your assistant, you go outside the room while the audience pick any telephone number.

When you return, by merely touching your assistant's head, you can reveal the number!

The secret lies in the way you rest your hands on your assistant's head. Here's the way to do it!

Your assistant can learn this secret in ten seconds, but your audience will take much longer to discover it!

Try this in front of a mirror to ensure perfection

The fingers cover the top joint of the jaw. By clenching her teeth and relaxing them, your assistant codes the number to you. You can _feel_ the impulses but the audience can't _see_ them. If the number is

4675

your assistant clenches her jaw <u>4</u> times, then pauses. Then <u>6</u> times — pause — <u>7</u> times — pause — <u>5</u> times — stop

THE HUMAN CLOCK

Here's another thought-reading trick. This time, you prove that you can read the time on a watch hidden in somebody's pocket.

(1) While you are out of the room, your friends set the hands on a watch to a time selected by themselves.

(2) When the watch has been hidden in a person's pocket, you return. You gaze into the person's eyes and are able to announce the time at which they have set the watch

SECRET — One of the people in the room is your secret confederate. It is he who has the watch hidden in his pocket. He codes the figures to you in ← this manner

```
1      2      3

4     [5]     6

7      8      9

10     11     12
```

(3) When he is facing you (that's you in the drawing!) he imagines that figures surround your head and simply looks in the direction of the right figure for the hour selected. (10, 11, & 12 are imagined as being right shoulder, heart, left shoulder — well away from head to avoid confusion with 7, 8 & 9)

(4) The minutes are coded by his hands. Each finger represents 10 minutes. If he has 4 fingers showing like this it means 40 minutes past the hour

COLOUR SENSE

In which you prove that you can "sense" colours with your finger tips!

All you need is —

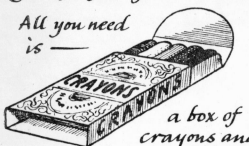

a box of crayons and — an audience.

When a friend has selected a crayon—

and placed it in your hand behind your back, you are able to tell him the colour of the crayon.

SECRET? It's so simple!

Although you **keep** the crayon behind your back (and the audience **sees** it there)

Crayon mark

you smear the crayon on your right hand **second** finger tip.

Then, when you turn to face your friend, you point to him with your first finger, and glimpse the crayon mark on your second finger, which is folded into your fist.

It's bold, but it works!

THE SILENT SPELLING BEE

All these things on the table — but you can show that you know which of them a person is thinking of!

Invite your friend to think of one of these articles when you have laid them on the table. Ask him to spell the name of the article silently — one letter at a time as you tap each article in turn. When he has reached the last letter he is to say "stop!" At that moment, your wand is already resting on the item he thought of!

SECRET!

Tap on any article for the first two taps. Then tap in this order:—

KEY	(spells with	3	letters)
CLIP	" "	4	"
WATCH	" "	5	"
PENCIL	" "	6	"
LIGHTER	" "	7	"
NOTECASE	" "	8	"
CIGARETTE	" "	9	"
TABLE CLOTH	" "	10	"
FOUNTAIN PEN	" "	11	"
HANDKERCHIEF	" "	12	"
CIGARETTE CASE	" "	13	"

To make this into a portable pocket mystery, cut out pictures of the articles (or of any other articles spelt with the correct number of letters) and paste them on paper. Try to take it further — up to 20 letters!

TWO—
for the price
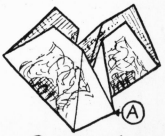
of — ONE

Two 10/-
notes?
It looks
like it, but
really it's only one

SECRET
— a trick fold!

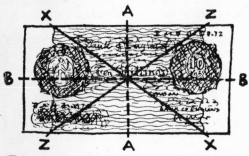

Fold away from you from
X to X and Z to Z (the borders
of the shaded centre portion).
Then fold towards you the
lines A-A and B-B,
(centre lines of the note)

Fold the note so —

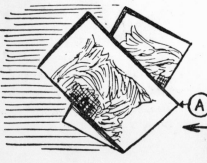

Press Ⓐ to the right, and
the corresponding fold at
the back to the left and —
there you have it!

SPECIAL EDITION! EXTRA!

Your audience will think it's a very special edition indeed when they see you tear the newspaper to shreds and restore it with a magic word!

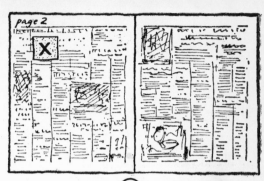

You'll need two copies of the same paper. Take the outside pages of each, and prepare one like this

① Paste is applied to square X on inside of page 2 in newspaper "A"

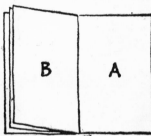

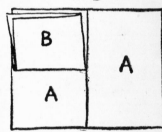

② Newspaper "B" is laid, face out, on newspaper "A", and pressed on pasted square shown with dotted lines at X.)

③ Right hand page of "B" is folded to left

④ Lower half of "B" is folded upwards

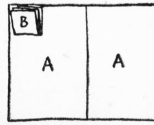

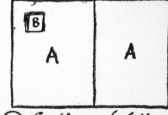

⑤ Right hand side of "B" is folded to left.

⑥ Lower half of packet "B" is folded upward

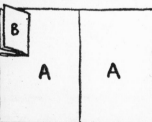

⑦ Continue folding until you have "B" in a small bundle, with edges folded in, stuck to back of "A"

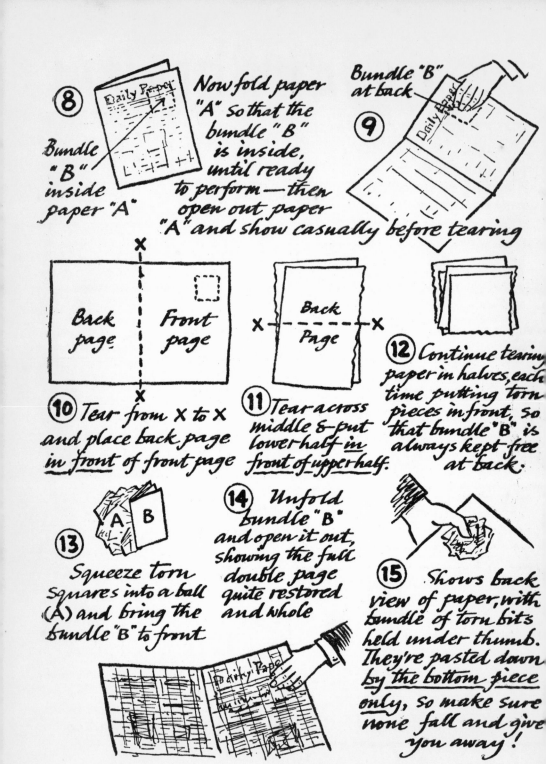

(8) Bundle "B" inside paper "A"

Now fold paper "A" so that the bundle "B" is inside, until ready to perform — then open out paper "A" and show casually before tearing

(9) Bundle "B" at back

Back page | Front page

Back Page

(10) Tear from X to X and place back page in front of front page

(11) Tear across middle & put lower half in front of upper half.

(12) Continue tearing paper in halves, each time putting torn pieces in front, so that bundle "B" is always kept free at back.

(13) Squeeze torn squares into a ball (A) and bring the bundle "B" to front

(14) Unfold bundle "B" and open it out, showing the full double page quite restored and whole

(15) Shows back view of paper, with bundle of torn bits held under thumb. They're pasted down by the bottom piece only, so make sure none fall and give you away!

THE RAJAH'S JEWELS

An ancient Hindu legend tells how a Rajah, whose jewels were accidentally flung into a river infested with crocodiles, offered half of them to any man who could recover them for him.

This clever trick shows you how to perform a similar miracle.

This bottle of water represents the river, and the brightly coloured beads play the part of the Rajah's jewels.

Here's how to get the "jewels" out without spilling the water

The beads (or "jewels") are steel ball bearings brightly painted.

The cork of the bottle contains a small but powerful bar magnet (obtainable from scientific supply houses)

After you have shown the bottle of water containing the "jewels" you place it behind your back.

A second or so later, you bring it forward again, with the beads extracted and held in the other hand.

When the bottle is behind your back, you extract the cork and gently run it up the outside of the bottle. The magnet carries the steel balls up to the mouth of the bottle and out.

Can you believe your eyes?

Use a piece of glass or Perspex rod like this ⟶ as an **"EYE-SIGHT TESTER"**

and you'll wonder whether you _can_ believe your eyes!

MAGIC!
MAGIC!

Hold the rod over these letters:—   and you see:—

CODE BOOK   **CODE BOOK**

Now look through the rod at these:—   and this is what you see:—

MAGIC MAN   **MAGIC MAN** (inverted)

Now try:—   Which appears as:—

CHOICE FRUIT   **CHOICE FRUIT** (inverted)

SECRET

The glass _inverts_ letters. Those that have the bottom half like the top half (BCDEHIKOX) are really inverted, although they don't seem to be. Work out more word "tests" like the above and ASTONISH YOUR FRIENDS NOW!

It's —

MOST AMAZING! ISN'T IT?

114

DICE DECEPTION

Have a member of your audience lay out a number of dice on the table, after rolling them at random.

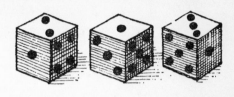

Without touching the dice, you can always tell him the number on the <u>under-side</u> of the dice.

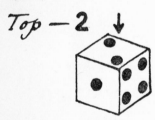

SECRET

The two opposite sides of all genuine dice <u>always</u> total **7**

Top — 2 ↓   Top — 1 ↓   Top — 3 ↓

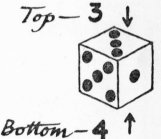

Bottom — 5 ↑   Bottom — 6 ↑   Bottom — 4 ↑

Remember, please! that if you only have one, it's a **DIE**. More than one, and the word is **DICE!** Audiences are quick to criticise incorrect English!

I ONLY CHEAT A LITTLE!

— That was the catch-phrase used by Paul Rosini, famous American Conjuror — "I only cheat a little!" And in this baffling mystery, _you_ cheat a little!

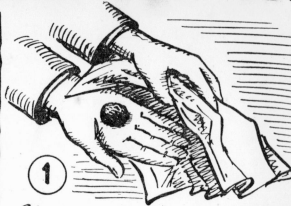

① Your audience see you place a walnut or other small article in your right hand, & cover it with a handkerchief.

② One by one, the spectators place their hands under the handkerchief to make sure the walnut is still there. When the last spectator has convinced himself that it's not vanished —

③ — you whip off the handkerchief and show that the walnut has gone! And although the spectators may search you thoroughly, they'll never find the walnut on you!

BECAUSE — Ssh! _You haven't got it!_ The last spectator to feel under the handkerchief was a confederate, & you had previously told him to _take the nut_ out of your hand when he felt under the handkerchief!

The BAFFLING BANANA

If you peeled a banana and found that it was already cut into neat pieces you'd think it rather odd, wouldn't you?

— So will your friends when you play this trick on them!

① Needle & cotton are threaded through peel

Section through banana

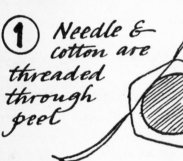

② Needle is pushed back into same hole and thread is taken further round until —

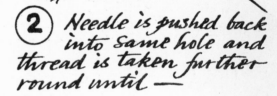

③ needle finally emerges through first hole again

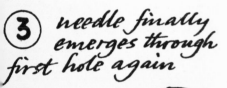

④ Both ends of thread are pulled out, cutting through banana but leaving peel intact!

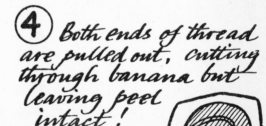

YOU CAN — THEY CAN'T

perform this little juggle with two cubes of sugar & a glass tumbler

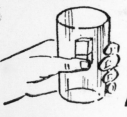

Thumb holds lump of sugar against glass, with another lump balanced on top of first.

PROBLEM — *to toss each lump, one at a time, into the air & catch it in the glass*

The first lump is easy to catch. But unless you know how, the second lump is harder. The necessary jerk will fling the first lump out of the glass!

SECRET

After catching first lump ___

① *Thumb leaves go of second lump*

② *Hand lowers glass rapidly before lump can fall —*

③ *and slips glass beneath the falling second lump*

④ *which simply drops into the glass!*

118

THE SUPER RING VANISH

A borrowed ring, covered with a handkerchief, vanishes completely!

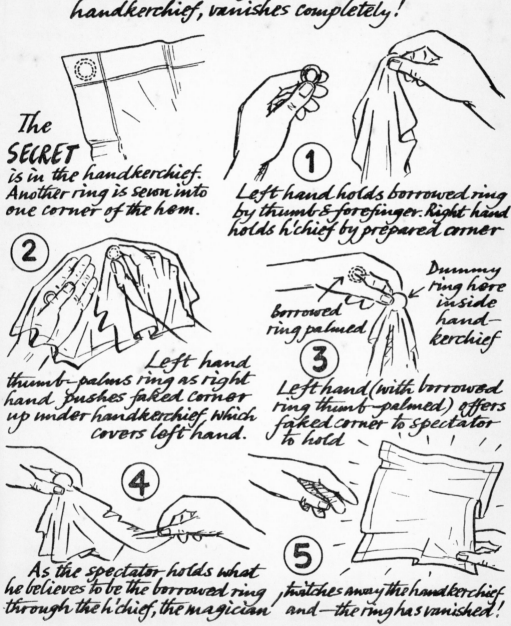

The **SECRET** is in the handkerchief. Another ring is sewn into one corner of the hem.

1 Left hand holds borrowed ring by thumb & forefinger. Right hand holds h'chief by prepared corner

2 Left hand thumb-palms ring as right hand pushes faked corner up under handkerchief, which covers left hand.

borrowed ring palmed

Dummy ring here inside handkerchief

3 Left hand (with borrowed ring thumb-palmed) offers faked corner to spectator to hold

4 As the spectator holds what he believes to be the borrowed ring through the h'chief, the magician

5 twitches away the handkerchief and — the ring has vanished!

THE RING AND THE

On your table the audience see a ball of wool resting on a large goblet or glass vase.

They see you borrow a lady's ring and make it vanish.

They see the lady unwind the wool and find her ring in the very middle of it.

BUT What they don't see is the way the ball of wool has been prepared for the trick!

Front view of ball of wool and goblet.

Side view showing flat tin funnel in ball of wool

Paint tube same colour as wool

This is the tin tube (actual size) through which the ring finds its way into the ball of wool

And this is the other bit of preparation needed — a ring sewn into the corner of your handkerchief.

BALL OF WOOL

In which you use the ring vanish already shown earlier in this book

Having borrowed the ring, gain possession of it by the **SUPER RING VANISH** method, in your left hand & grip it in thumb-crotch

1 Right hand puts ball of wool into left, placing tube over palmed ring

2 Left hand turns ball over, allowing ring to fall down tube

3 Left hand holds end of tube in thumb grip as right hand pulls ball of wool off tube—

4 Leaving tube concealed in left hand as right hand pops ball of wool on glass. Ring is now inside ball.

5 The lady unwinds the wool by pulling on the end, & the ring clinks into the glass as the last turn of wool is unwound.

HOW TO PUT THE TUBE IN THE BALL OF WOOL

Just start the ball on one end of the tube by wrapping wool round & round, until a big ball is formed, leaving end of tube projecting.

FULL — EMPTY!

One minute this packet of cigarettes is full. The next, and it's empty. Yet nobody has taken any out!

① Take out the tray from the pocket and cut right across it one inch from the bottom.

Cut

② Replace both halves of tray in outer packet & fill with cigarettes. Leave top projecting a little so that you can grip it with your fingers.

Line of cut on inner tray

WATCH THE ANGLES!

③ When you push the tray up from the bottom you push up the tray with it and the box is seen to be full.

Cigarettes stay behind

④ But when you pull the tray up from the top, the cigarettes are left behind in the packet — which seems to be empty

The Topsy-Turvy Bottle

  You stand a bottle upside-down and cover it with a paper tube. When you take off the tube the bottle is standing right way up!

1 Cut — You'll need two of those cardboard imitation bottles that novelty gifts are packed in. Cut them in half as shown by the heavy line.

2 Glue the two top halves together, and make a tube of shiny black paper. Stick a label on each side, one upside-down, the other right way up

Labels — Tube is tight fit on bottle

3 Black tube shaded →  By sliding the black tube up or down you can make the bottle seem upside-down, or right way up. At start, black tube is pushed up, and bottle appears to be upside-down.

Paper tube — **4** Roll up a piece of stiff paper into a larger tube, place it over trick bottle, and in doing so force down the shiny black tube. Bottle will now appear right way up.

SOLID WATER!

You may already know the old trick in which you fill a glass with water, place a piece of paper over the mouth of the glass, & turn the full glass upside down without spilling the water.

Do you know how to take the paper away — still without spilling the water?

 You need a wine glass, with a foot the same diameter as the mouth of the glass

You also need a thin disc of clear celluloid the same size as the foot of the glass.  *disc*

---

① Wet the disc and it will stick to the foot of the glass until wanted ➔

② Fill the glass and stand it on your left hand — disc & all

---

③  Take glass in right hand and place left hand (containing disc) on top of glass.

④ Take off left hand, leaving disc on glass, & lay paper over disc.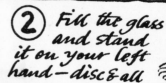

---

⑤  Replace left hand over paper & turn glass upside down.

⑥ Now, steadily, take paper away from the side. The disc holds the water in safely!

A Quart into a Pint Pot

It _can_ be done this way! But it's just as convincing to demonstrate the fact with two wine glasses.

Wineglass No 1. is full to the brim with water

Wineglass No. 2 is filled with pins.

Fill No 1 glass _very carefully_ with a thin stream of water, so as to avoid wetting the rim

Level of water will rise in a noticeable "hump" over glass top as the pins are added one by one. More than 300 pins can be put in the glass of water without it overflowing!

THE SANDS OF THE DESERT

Dry sand is poured into a bowl of water—

the magician scoops out a handful—

and immediately is able to change the wet mass into dry sand!

(1) Fry the sand in a clean pan until it's hot enough to scorch a piece of white paper laid on it.

(2) Now add 1 inch of wax candle to the sand. Let it melt, and stir it well into the sand.

(3) The sand will come out of the pan in a solid lump when cold. But it can be crumbled easily.

It's now waterproof, and you're ready to produce your miracle!

WATER BECOMES WINE!

In this good old favourite trick, clear water poured from a jug becomes wine or water, just as you wish!

The jug and the four glasses you use must be prepared beforehand. Here is—

THE SECRET

Glass No 1. has a few drops of PHENOLPHTHALEIN in it

Glass No 2. has nothing in it

Glass No 3. has a few drops of PHENOLPHTHALEIN in it

Glass No 4. has a few drops of TARTARIC ACID dissolved in water

The jug Contains a small quantity of SODIUM CARBONATE dissolved in water.

1st Pouring. 1 & 3 look like wine, 2 & 4 are clear. Jug is clear.

2nd Pouring. Glasses 1, 2 & 3, when put back into jug, turn jug's contents into "wine"

Alternative Pouring. Pour all 4 glasses back into jug, and all the liquid becomes clear, like water.

THE RESTLESS BALL

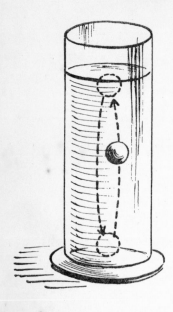

A small white ball rises to the top and sinks to the bottom of a tall glass vase — not once but over & over again — rising, sinking, rising sinking, rising & sinking.

This is the ball

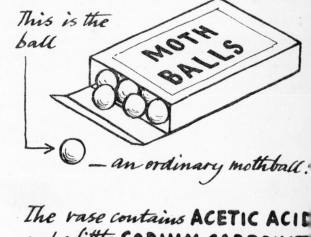

— an ordinary mothball:

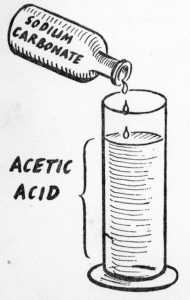

The vase contains ACETIC ACID and a little SODIUM CARBONATE which generates a gas. The bubbles of the gas cause the mothball to rise to the surface At the surface, the bubbles burst, and the ball sinks It collects more bubbles, rises — but you know the rest by now, don't you?

DRY WATER — BY MAGIC!

If you could prove that wet water was dry, you'd be a magician indeed, wouldn't you?

HERE'S THE SECRET —

(1) When a magician — that's you! — dips his hand in water and brings it out DRY, it means that he has secretly

(2) Sprinkled the surface of the water with a chemical powder called LICOPODIUM which you may buy at your local chemist's shop.

(3) This powder spreads invisibly on the surface of the water & forms a barrier which S-T-R-E-T-C-H-E-S to allow the hand to be dipped in the bowl. The hand never really touches the water, which is kept from it by the invisible licopodium film.

FLOATING SUGAR

It's disconcerting, to say the least, when the sugar you pop in your tea floats merrily instead of dissolving — as respectable sugar should !

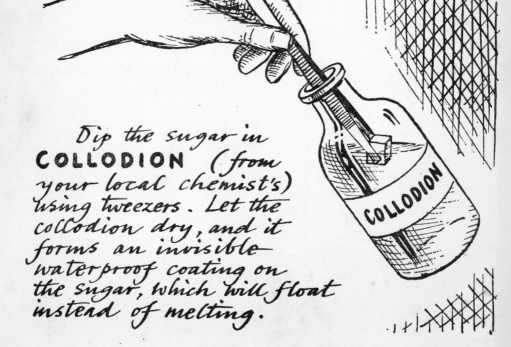

Dip the sugar in **COLLODION** (from your local chemist's) using tweezers. Let the collodion dry, and it forms an invisible waterproof coating on the sugar, which will float instead of melting.

PHANTOM SMOKE

As the smoke from a burning taper vanishes into the air at one side of the stage, it is seen to reappear in a glass vase at the other side of the stage.

These two chemicals produce smoke when their fumes mix.

3 drops of AMMONIA are smeared inside the lid of the vase.

3 drops of HYDROCHLORIC ACID (Spirits of Salt, or Muriatic Acid) are swished round the inside of the vase.

Keep lid face-down and well away from the vase. Then the fumes won't mix until you are ready to do the trick.

BOTH THESE LIQUIDS AND THEIR FUMES ARE **DANGEROUS** BE CAREFUL!

As soon as the lid is placed on the vase, smoke-like fumes start to appear.

131

ATOMIC
BUBBLES

Blowing bubbles that
explode with a bright
flash is a magic trick,
and not a children's
game ! **BE CAREFUL** when you perform this mystery!

Piece of
wire gauze

Cotton wool
Soaked in
petrol

Preparation of pipe
for blowing
Atomic Bubbles

Bubble mixture
is made with
soapsuds and
glycerine (which
makes bubbles
stronger)

A lighted
cigarette or taper
is used to explode
the bubbles.

MAGIC SPRINGTIME!

From
White snow — to — Green
Springtime
using a lighted match for sunshine!

Paint sky blue, and all other shaded portions and lines brown.

All white portions are painted over with a solution of COBALT CHLORIDE.

Leave picture to dry. When it is exposed to the heat of a lighted match, the white portions change to green. And to bring back the snow — just breathe on the picture. It will turn white again!

The Human Power Plant

If you could take a light bulb from its socket and make it light up brightly while you held it in your hand, you'd be a magician!

Here's the **SECRET**

— one of those miniature key-ring electric torches

Torch gripped by third and fourth fingers. Fourth finger exerts twist to switch on torch

Side view of hand, showing how to hold bulb and torch

IMPORTANT!
① Always use a frosted bulb
② **PRACTISE WELL!**

The Colour-Changing Balloon

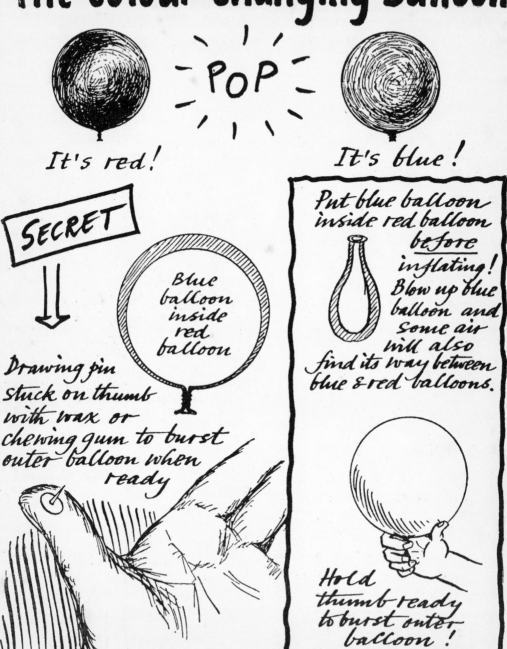

It's red!

POP

It's blue!

SECRET

Blue balloon inside red balloon

Drawing pin stuck on thumb with wax or chewing gum to burst outer balloon when ready

Put blue balloon inside red balloon *before* inflating! Blow up blue balloon and some air will also find its way between blue & red balloons.

Hold thumb ready to burst outer balloon!

THE GHOSTS' GALLERY

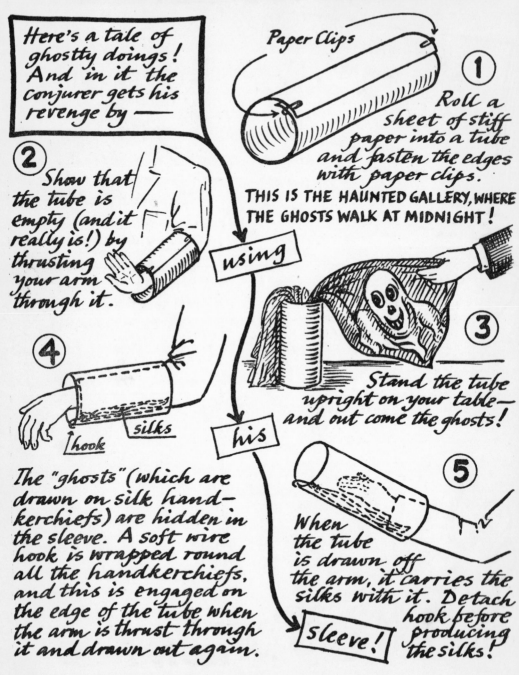

Here's a tale of ghostly doings! And in it the conjurer gets his revenge by —

Paper Clips

① Roll a sheet of stiff paper into a tube and fasten the edges with paper clips.

THIS IS THE HAUNTED GALLERY, WHERE THE GHOSTS WALK AT MIDNIGHT!

② Show that the tube is empty (and it really is!) by thrusting your arm through it.

using

③ Stand the tube upright on your table — and out come the ghosts!

④ hook   silks

his

The "ghosts" (which are drawn on silk hand-kerchiefs) are hidden in the sleeve. A soft wire hook is wrapped round all the handkerchiefs, and this is engaged on the edge of the tube when the arm is thrust through it and drawn out again.

⑤ When the tube is drawn off the arm, it carries the silks with it. Detach hook before producing the silks!

sleeve!

What? No Juice?

This is a colourful trick that goes down well at a party. Known as "The Ribbon from the Orange," it was a great favourite with that grand conjurer, the late David Devant.

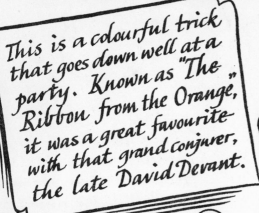

From a bowl of oranges, one is selected and marked by a member of the audience, and given to the magician, who makes passes over it with his magic wand.

Then he nicks the peel, and from the orange extracts yards — and — yards — and — yards — and yards of brightly coloured ribbon —.

HOW?

HERE'S THE SECRET→

This little device, prepared beforehand, threads a long, stout needle through the orange

④

Needle

Tightly coiled ribbon

⑤ Ribbon is threaded through eye of needle and coiled tightly. End of ribbon is lightly gummed to coil. The coil, with needle pointed outwards, is palmed in your left hand. The orange is forced on to the needle point & pressed down. Make a slit in orange with a knife, and pull out needle — the ribbon will follow!

End is lightly gummed to coil

⑥

Orange is spiked on needle

Here's a useful tip: — use a TANGERINE ORANGE for easier working!

THE CONFETTI TUBE

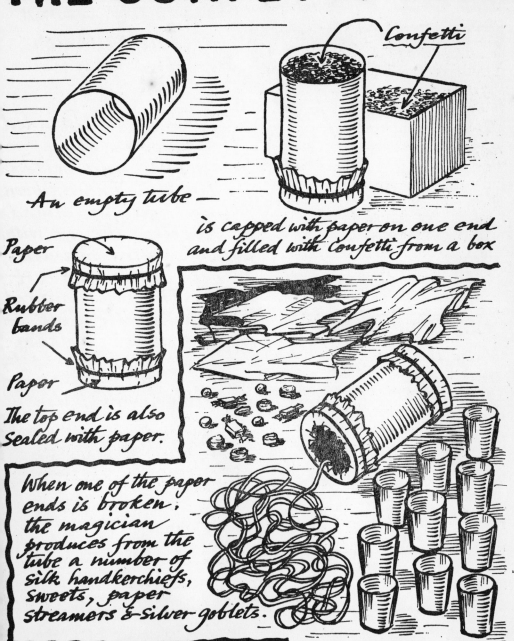

An empty tube —

is capped with paper on one end
and filled with confetti from a box

Confetti

Paper

Rubber
bands

Paper

The top end is also
sealed with paper.

When one of the paper
ends is broken,
the magician
produces from the
tube a number of
silk handkerchiefs,
sweets, paper
streamers & silver goblets.

 **THE SECRET** is inside the box of Confetti.

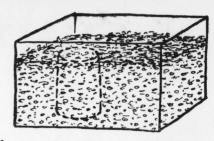

The largest silver goblet, which contains the load to be produced, is hidden by the confetti in the box.

The goblets are nested together

paper coil of streamers

— silks

— sweets

Paper disc

Largest goblet, when loaded, has a paper disc gummed on mouth

The tube is made to be a tight fit over largest goblet

In filling tube with confetti, the magician places it in the confetti box for a moment. The tube is guided on to goblet, which breaks paper seal on tube. But, the paper disc on mouth of goblet takes the place of paper on tube when tube is taken out and shown.

At finish tube is shown, quite empty! The audience will only find an empty tube with the two paper seals, and two rubber bands. The load is its own Container!

THE SPIRITS' BOX

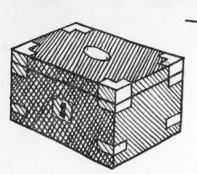

— which can be shown quite empty whenever you wish, but from which you can extract an enormous load.

The box is shown empty by tipping it forward and opening the lid. What could be fairer?

Box upright

Audience's view →

PIVOT

Box tilted forward.

Audience's view →

PIVOT

The box (which has no bottom) has a pivotting inner container, as shown in these end-view sections. The inner container stays put when the box is tilted forward. <u>Side</u> of container appears as <u>bottom</u> of box

Audience's view ↙

Back view of box showing load chamber when box is tilted forward to show "empty"

The CHEST of the GENII

This is an easily made box which appears to be empty but from which you can produce silks, flags, streamers and ribbons.

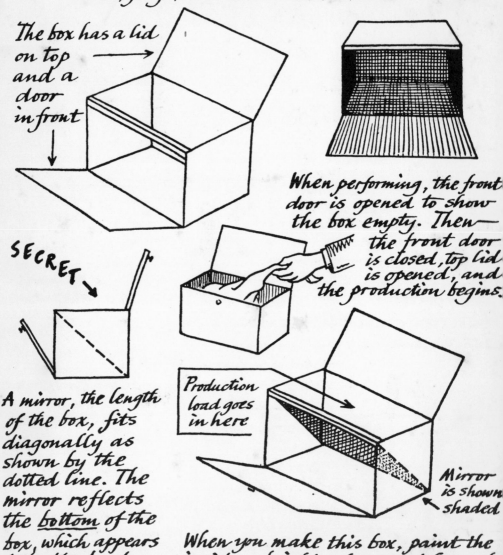

The box has a lid on top and a door in front

When performing, the front door is opened to show the box empty. Then the front door is closed, top lid is opened, and the production begins.

SECRET→

A mirror, the length of the box, fits diagonally as shown by the dotted line. The mirror reflects the <u>bottom</u> of the box, which appears to be the <u>back</u> of the box.

Production load goes in here

Mirror is shown shaded

When you make this box, paint the inside a <u>bright</u> colour, and have the outside a good contrasting colour.

The RABBIT out of the HAT

Here it is — magic's most famous and best-loved trick! Magicians know many methods of producing a rabbit from a hat. Here's just one way —

EMPTY!

After showing the hat empty, the magician places it on his table while he takes off his coat, to prove that there are no rabbits there!

He then picks up the hat, and produces the bunny! Simple, isn't it?

When the conjurer picks up the hat he slips his thumb in the large ring and the bag swings into the hat as he turns it over. He slips out the securing thread and — there's the bunny!

The SECRET is simple, too

The rabbit is concealed in a black cloth bag, hanging on a headless nail behind the table. The bag has a wide mouth which is closed by a stout thread run through eyelets. It hangs by a large ring.

Table is here seen in side view

WARNING!

Never, never pick up a rabbit by the ears. Always grasp it by the loose skin at the back of the neck